N
8550
.B88

Burns, J. T.

Framing pictures

6.95

DATE			

Framing pictures

J. T. Burns

Framing pictures

Charles Scribner's Sons · New York

cy 6

1 3 5 7 9 11 13 15 17 19 I/C 20 18 16 14 12 10 8 6 4 2
Printed in Great Britain

Library of Congress Catalog Card No: 77–83674
ISBN 0–684–15509–5 (cased)
      0–684–15508–7 (paper) SL 767

Contents

Introduction

Although this book is written mainly as a guide to the methods and techniques used for picture framing, I have also striven to indicate some idea of the aesthetic considerations that make so much difference between a well-made frame and a well-framed picture.

The reader who is already a skilled woodworker will need very little of the technical guidance given here to produce a beautifully made frame, but I hope he will find more than the bare bones of measuring, cutting and joining to interest him.

Many artists, not only those driven by the harsh economics of their vocation, but those with their own special ideas of framing, will also, I hope, find some practical help in these pages.

There are so many ways of framing any one subject out of such an enormous variety of material that it is difficult to think of anything offering more scope for creative self-expression. Indeed, because it is a pursuit that constantly encourages the close observation of the visual arts and their presentation, there can be no more rewarding or pleasant way of developing both hand and eye than framing pictures.

1 Early 14th-century triptych. (Duccio *Virgin and child with saints.*
Reproduced by courtesy of the Trustees, The National Gallery, London)

1 The influence of history

Modern printing techniques have fostered a universal interest in art by making available a profusion of sumptuously illustrated books and colour reproductions of paintings and drawings, from the earliest known cave-paintings to the most recent abstractions. Rarely, however, is a Rembrandt painting or a work by Dürer illustrated in the frame in which it has probably been displayed for hundreds of years. Indeed, unless you have the good fortune to see original works in the leading museums and art galleries, you will have little conception of how they are presented for public display.

It is generally supposed that paintings by great masters are kept in their original frames where possible, or are at least framed in the style of their period and place of origin. While this is, sadly, not always so, it remains the criterion expected by most people who share an interest in the visual arts, and you can usually find paintings in their appropriate and historical setting in art galleries and great houses. Here the influence of history and tradition can be seen as much in the framing of pictures as in the pictures themselves, up to and including the present day. Architecture, classical form and decoration, fashion and furniture all played an important part, with the skilled craftsman interpreting and, indeed, often inspiring the infinite variety of design until, with the coming of the Industrial Revolution and the first signs of mass-production, he was forced to assume a secondary role.

The earliest frames probably date from the Middle Ages when panel paintings, usually subordinate to church architecture, were enclosed by a raised rim of the panel. In the thirteenth century, paintings became separate and movable entities with their frames ornately carved and decorated and sometimes detachable from the painted panel. These medieval panel paintings were church altarpieces, usually in the form of hinged compartments: a *diptych* with two panels, a *triptych* with three panels, or a *polyptych* with many panels, supported by a narrow base called the *predella*. The best known form is the triptych (fig. 1); the large central panel usually depicts the Madonna and Child, and pictures of the saints are painted on the side panels which, being half the width of the centre panel, can be folded to close and protect the paintings. The carving and ornamentation of these altarpieces is essentially gothic, following the architectural style predominant in Northern Europe for about four hundred years from the twelfth century.

The influence of Gothic art was also strong in Italy until the fifteenth century which saw the momentous Italian Renaissance and the works of great masters such as Michelangelo, Raphael and Leonardo. Innovations in painting were accompanied by new styles of framing. The frame now became a completely separate unit, carved, gilded and coloured in har-

PORTRAIT OF A GIRL. STUDIO OF DOMENICO GHIRLANDAIO C.A. 1448-1494

3

2 15th-century Italian Renaissance frame. (Studio of Domenico Ghirlandaio *Portrait of a girl*. Reproduced by courtesy of the Trustees, The National Gallery, London)

3 17th-century Spanish frame with deep carving. (Juan de Valdés-Leal *The Virgin of the Immaculate Conception*. Courtauld Institute Galleries, London)

4 Elaborately carved French frame of the 17th century. (Poussin *Adoration of the Golden Calf*. Reproduced by courtesy of the Trustees, The National Gallery, London)

▶

4

mony with the painting. Frame-makers took less heed of architectural and religious motifs and preferred natural forms derived from flowers and foliage. The revival of ancient Greek and Roman art which influenced Italian painting of this period was in turn reflected in the frame-maker's craft. Despite the ever-changing and inspired variety of ornamentation, the basic design of these frames remained fairly constant for two hundred years and has been a major influence in framing paintings to this day. It comprises a gilded, reeded or patterned moulding around the painting, then a wider flat panel embossed, painted or decorated with various designs, and an outer moulding similar to the inner one (fig. 2). Frequently the inner and outer mouldings consist of a running pattern of leaves or similar ornament with perhaps a flower pattern decorating the corners of the frame.

From the sixteenth century the influence of Italian paintings and the manner in which they were framed was very great, notably in Spain, France and Germany; but each country including the whole of northern Europe showed its own characteristic idiom: the deep bold carving of the Spanish (fig. 3), the highly imaginative decoration of the French, or the incredibly detailed and precise carving of the Germans are typical of the period.

During the seventeenth century the styles known as mannerism and baroque, both emanating from Italy, affected architecture and painting. The mannerist style, restless and often grotesque, is seen in many frames of the early part of this period and the exuberance of the later Roman baroque is also still in evidence.

By this time, leadership in the visual arts in Europe was shifting from Italy to France where, in the second half of the seventeenth century, the arbiter of style and taste was the Sun King, Louis XIV of France, whose court became the focus of all the decorative arts, especially furniture and interior design. The French Louis XIV frame remains well-known today and has been much copied in spite of, or perhaps because of, a certain standardization of the form at this period. The carving is florid, elaborate and stylized with corner and centre designs strongly accentuated and, of course, gilded overall (fig. 4).

Although the French influence was felt in Holland, the splendid Dutch school of painting flourished quite independently of the rest of Europe and frames of equal originality were made by Dutch craftsmen for these great paintings. Perhaps the most important feature of seventeenth-century Dutch frames was the use of wood, especially the fruit woods, oak and ebony, the beauty of the wood itself being the dominant feature. These frames, so often associated with the works of Rembrandt, de Hooch and Vermeer, are frequently painted entirely black; the carving is simple with perhaps interlacing wavy bands and, where gilding or colouring is used, it is minimal (fig. 5).

In England, many factors influenced the development of frames: Italian, French and Dutch styles were all copied assiduously by highly skilled

5

5 17th-century Dutch frame. (Vermeer *The Guitar Player*. The Iveagh
Bequest, Kenwood, London)

carvers and gilders. Grinling Gibbons, Master Carver in Wood to Charles II, is often quoted as being among the greatest woodcarvers who ever lived. Later, Thomas Chippendale was also to make his original contribution to the design of frames with carving that, notably in the Chinese-inspired idiom of his day, can only be described as fantastic. Mirrors were particularly fashionable in carved and gilded frames, sometimes of amazing complexity (fig. 6).

Until the second half of the eighteenth century, exuberance was the keynote of both visual and purely decorative art in most of Europe. It gave way to a movement, once more initiated in Italy, known as neoclassicism, which soon influenced the whole of the civilized world. This classical revival is exemplified in the etchings of Piranesi in Italy and the paintings of David in France. Frames again echoed the innovation using simple, reeded lines, plain slopes with pearls (or 'shot') nearest the picture, with sometimes an undulating ribbon motif nearest the raised outer edge. Such frames are often known as Louis XVI pattern.

The early years of the nineteenth century produced the Empire frame, a style with overtones of Napoleon and his Egyptian campaigns. Lotus, palm-leaves and papyrus motifs were introduced into frame designs, following the general Empire style of the period, and paintings in France were often forced willy-nilly into these frames which became a kind of Napoleonic uniform for works of art.

The great leap forward of nineteenth-century industrialism meant the almost total eclipse of the woodcarver's skill in favour of the moulded plaster frame. These frames, often given euphemistic names such as 'Barbizon' or Louis this or that, were usually heavy, clumsy and sometimes quite nasty copies of the exquisitely carved frames of the seventeenth and eighteenth centuries. In England, plaster or composition copies of the Louis XIV frame described earlier were made at an enormous rate, and a simulated gold-leaf, made from brass and bronze powder mixtures, was the most widely used finish. Even today, no old-established corporation board room is complete without its Victorian portrait of the beloved founder in its 'period' (plaster) frame.

There were, however, a number of significant and even revolutionary changes in framing which did not derive from a royal court or an architectural or decorative fashion. Painters themselves sought ways of framing their work to suit their new vision. Many of the French Impressionists used plain white frames of extreme simplicity. Seurat used coloured dots all over some of his frames, echoing his particular technique of accentuating colour contrast in his paintings.

6 Mirror in a carved gilt frame, English, mid 18th century. (Victoria and Albert Museum. Crown Copyright)

7 A typical 'Whistler' frame, designed by the artist. (Whistler *Old Battersea Bridge*. The Tate Gallery, London)

The Pre-Raphaelites in England designed many of their own frames, some of which were superbly carved and gilded, the influence of William Morris being much in evidence. Rossetti's painting *The Blessed Damozel* is framed in a manner reminiscent of medieval architecture with gothic columns and a painted predella (fig. 8). James McNeill Whistler who, in spite of his association with European art, was American, designed frames which some painters admire greatly today. His designs varied, but the 'Whistler frame' is usually painted black and reeded in wide receding steps from the highest point nearest the picture (fig. 7).

THE BLESSED DAMOZEL

8 19th-century Pre-Raphaelite frame. (Rossetti *The Blessed Damozel*. Lady Lever Collection, Port Sunlight)

21

Simplicity, even severity, has become much the theme in framing as the twentieth century progresses, a hard-edge form of presentation being well suited to abstract art and many daring modern methods of painting. This has undoubtedly given rise to the present-day fashion for metal angle frames for almost any kind of painting, print or poster, whether or not they bear any relation to the style of the picture.

There are also some kinds of presentation (which cannot strictly be called framing, because the idea is to avoid the frame) in which the picture is sandwiched between acrylic sheet (Perspex or Plexiglass) or glass and a hardboard (Masonite) backing by means of metal or plastic clips, or by simply sticking the picture onto a thick piece of block-board and varnishing the surface. All these methods are popular, deservedly or not, and will be discussed later.

In the art world of today it is interesting to see not only the influence of history in the framing of pictures but also, sometimes, the rejection of all tradition to a point where the *avant-garde* painter's vast canvas is considered to need only the whitewashed gallery wall to frame it – a curious analogy, perhaps, to art in the Stone Age which knew only the wall of the cave.

2 Materials and equipment

Framing a picture is not unlike furnishing a room. You may follow the fashion of the moment, or you may prefer a period style. But as the furniture must suit the scale and character of the room, so the frame must suit the picture. Whatever you choose will reflect your judgement and discrimination and finally bear the stamp of your personality.

The first and most important material to consider is the MOULDING. Thanks to modern technology in the milling, shaping and finishing of timber, an enormous range of picture-frame mouldings, prepared ready for use, is now available. These 'prepared' mouldings (as distinct from a frame made entirely by hand, including the finish of gold-leaf and colour) usually come in lengths of about 9ft (3m), in styles ranging from antique and traditional to the latest modern shapes (see colour illustration on page 37). A variety of metals, mostly extruded aluminium anodized in several finishes, and also brass and chrome-steel, is widely used for framing, the shape almost invariably conforming to a simple 90° angle. A more recent innovation is a thin-gauge metal skin wrapped around a wood moulding,

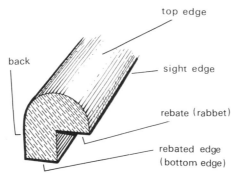

9 A simple half-round moulding showing the different parts referred to in the text.

leaving the rebate (see fig. 9) uncovered so that it can be glued and pinned in the normal way. There are also kits consisting of wood, metal and even plastic extrusions for home assembly which are simple enough to put together but depend on the picture fitting one of the range of available sizes.

The first problem for the beginner is what mouldings to buy and where to find them. Obviously the best place is a friendly picture-framer's shop or studio where there is bound to be a large and interesting range of materials and activity and where, hopefully, the professional framer takes kindly to the amateur and is willing to sell him some of the materials of his trade. In most large towns there are specialist suppliers of picture-frame

23

mouldings whose stocks include a variety of patterns from many parts of the world. Most of these wholesalers are not averse to selling small quantities to the non-professional. Your choice will be greatly simplified if, by some stratagem, you can acquire a copy of the wholesaler's illustrated catalogue. Various mouldings are, of course, used in the building and furnishing trades for trimming doors, windows, furniture and so on. The range is restricted but, being mass-produced, very much cheaper and easily come by. No rebate is made for these mouldings but this can be formed by adding a wooden fillet to the base (fig. 10).

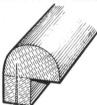

10 A half-round beading obtainable from a timber supplier, with a wooden fillet glued and pinned to form a rebate (rabbet).

A frame is made by joining four pieces of moulding, each cut at both ends at opposing angles of 45°, and it is the accuracy of this cut (the MITRE) upon which so much depends (see chapter 3). Obviously, if all measurements are correct and the mitred corners truly accurate, the frame will be absolutely square and firm; but if there is the slightest error in measurement or in the cutting of the mitres, the result is a wobbly and frail piece of handiwork. You will therefore need a good quality RULER, either the ordinary carpenter's folding type or a pull-out metal tape, and – of primary importance – a reliable and accurate device for cutting the mitres. The simplest and cheapest of many available types is the MITRE-BLOCK. This is usually of beech-wood with a base to which is secured an upright section with slotted guides for the saw to cut the two opposing 45° angled mitres. There is also a centre slot at right-angles to the edge of the block for sawing a 90° cut (fig. 11). The MITRE-BOX is similar to the mitre-block but has two

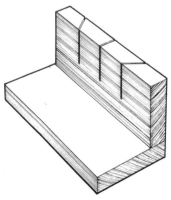

11 The simplest form of mitre-block.

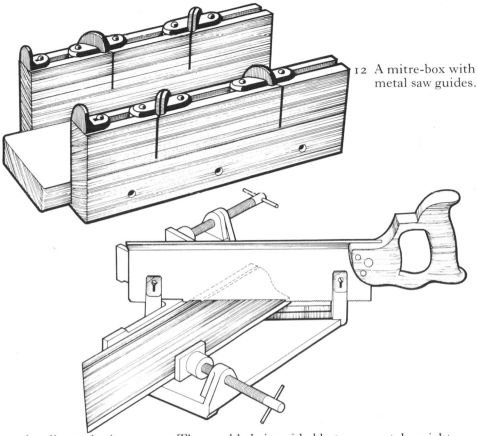

12 A mitre-box with metal saw guides.

13 An all-metal mitre-cutter. The saw blade is guided between metal uprights which incorporate adjustable stops for depth of cut. Two screw clamps grip the moulding at the required angles for cutting and mitres.

upright slotted sections (fig. 12) to afford greater stability to the saw. If you have never sawn wood at a precise angle before, the mitre-block is the cheapest and surest way to find out whether you are a potential wizard with the tenon saw or whether you need to consider a much more expensive but surer way of cutting the mitre accurately. There are a number of metal MITRE-CUTTERS which incorporate features that ensure that the moulding is firmly clamped and that all the angled corners are in register (fig. 13). Much hangs upon your choice of this piece of equipment and the only recommendation I would make is that you choose as wisely as your pocket and experience allow.

There is a machine called a MORSO CUTTER which consists of a foot-operated guillotine with a built-in measuring device and a pair of hollow-ground steel blades so arranged as to cut both opposing mitres in the same operation. Although excellent, it can only be of academic interest to the amateur unless, perhaps, he belongs to a group wealthy enough to establish a really well-equipped workshop for collective use.

You will need a WORK BENCH; it should be firm and solid, preferably of heavy timber with a top stout enough to accommodate a VICE bolted firmly to it. An engineer's vice, rather than the more usual carpenter's version, is recommended, as it is better suited for gripping the rebate of the moulding at the best height above the bench.

A light-weight (the lighter the better) pistol-grip ELECTRIC DRILL is almost essential, especially as it enables the drilling of pilot holes with one hand while the other holds the moulding in position, but you may find a sharp-pointed BRADAWL (which you will want for general use) quite adequate, at least for small mouldings. Some drill-bits, $\frac{1}{32}$in., $\frac{1}{16}$in. and $\frac{3}{32}$in. diameter, will be required for the electric drill. A hand-drill, because it requires two hands to operate it, is not recommended for picture-framing.

For making frames you will also need a good quality TENON SAW (sometimes called a back saw in the USA), 12ins (30cm) long, 4ins (10cm) deep, with 14 teeth to the inch; BRADS, variously called nails, gimp-pins or veneer pins in a small range of sizes for joining the frame and fitting the picture – a useful range would be $\frac{1}{2} \times 19$, $\frac{3}{4} \times 18$, 1×18, $1\frac{1}{4} \times 16$, $1\frac{1}{2} \times 16$ and $1\frac{3}{4} \times 16$ (length in inches × thickness in Standard Wire Gauge); a 10-oz. HAMMER, about right for joining the frame, though an even lighter one is best for fitting the picture.

Modern resin-based ADHESIVES are marvellous for frame-making, as no preparation such as heating is necessary. For purposes other than woodworking, however, the cellulose and starch-based adhesives should be used, for reasons which will be discussed in chapter 4.

The mount – known in the USA as 'mat' – is the cardboard margin around a picture, used generally for framing watercolours, all kinds of drawings, prints and similar works displayed under glass. MOUNTING (MATTING) BOARD is available in an almost bewildering range, but at this stage I would urge restraint and advise you not to buy more than one or two boards which are neutral in colour and which allow the picture to dominate the arrangement whatever its colour or tone. In chapter 4 I shall discuss the importance of the most careful choice of mounting boards and their colours and textures in a variety of applications. To start with, and indeed as a general rule, the very palest cream and beige tints are almost invariably safe and effective for mounting pictures and are available from art stores and suppliers.

A KNIFE is in constant demand and its point must always be razor sharp. Choose one with a good stout handle that can be grasped firmly in the fist when necessary. The type with replaceable blades is a great blessing (a Stanley knife in the UK, an X-Acto knife in the USA); the only thing worse than working with a blunt blade is having to sharpen it on a stone. A knife I particularly like consists of a comfortably proportioned handle accommodating a long blade divided into snap-off segments (fig. 14), providing a new knife-point each time the blunted segment is discarded. A special kind of blade is required by most framers for cutting the angled bevel of the mount. Mount-cutting is something of an individual problem which will

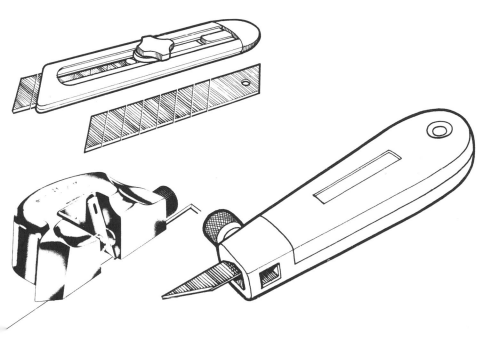

14 (*above*) A sturdy, economical knife. The blade has eight segments and can be released from the handle so that the blunted segment can be snapped off to give a new cutting edge.

15 (*right*) An excellent mount-cutting knife: a pad-saw handle fitted with an arrow-headed blade.

16 (*below*) The Dexter mat-cutter.

be fully explored in chapter 4. My own preference after much trial is a No.5903 Stanley blade gripped in a PAD-SAW HANDLE; the screw-grip for the blade is positive and quick in operation, and the shape of the handle is just right for the fistful of controlled cutting power needed (fig. 15).

For cutting mounts a STEEL STRAIGHT-EDGE is necessary to guide the blade (although many experts use simply a length of bevelled mounting board). I would recommend a straight-edge about 36ins (1m) long and 2ins (5cm) wide, with one side bevelled. The thickness of the steel can be something less than ⅛in. (3mm). Let me warn the beginner straight away of the danger of cutting against the *bevelled* side of the straight-edge except for the purpose and in the manner described on page 42.

There is a mount cutter which I have tried to use but which, perhaps to my shame rather than the maker's, did not fulfil its promise although I know it is quite widely and successfully used. I illustrate it (fig. 16) because it is the only small aid to mount-cutting that I have come across. A blade is clamped in the cutter at the required angle and depth of cut so that the instrument can be pushed along against a straight-edge guide of any kind to ensure a straight bevelled cut.

There is also a machine for cutting mounts which requires little skill or experience, but its high cost makes it impracticable for the amateur except, perhaps, in a group workshop where the expense might be justified. The bevelled edge is cut by a blade running against a calibrated stop which ensures the precise width of the four margins.

GLASS is a basic requirement for many kinds of framing and there is no reason why you should not learn to cut it to the sizes you need; but the beginner ought not to attempt handling glass in large sheets, as this is fraught with danger. A small unseen flaw can result in a terrifying shattering of the whole sheet while you are manoeuvring it with arms wide apart and hands holding the edges. The experienced glass worker, always mindful of such a catastrophe, backs calmly and neatly away from the jagged heap crashing at his feet. For my part, I am a dedicated coward where glass is concerned and I avoid working with pieces much bigger than 3ft (1m) square. Off-cuts about this size will prove adequate for most of the glazing you will want to do. Except for very large pictures, you will need light-weight picture-glass, 18oz. per square foot (2mm thick); window glass is 24oz. (3mm) and plate glass, such as that used for shop windows, is 32oz. (4mm). Some people like to use non-reflecting glass which is certainly effective but which, in my view, loses the precious quality that glass should impart to a picture.

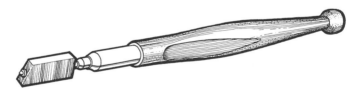

17 A glazier's diamond, for cutting picture glass.

For cutting light-weight picture glass, the GLAZIER'S DIAMOND (fig. 17) is much the best instrument although more expensive than the steel revolving wheel cutter which is said to be easier to handle at first. Once you have mastered the technique, and provided you allow no one but yourself to use it, the diamond will repay its initial cost many times over.

Most pictures, apart from paintings on canvas, need a BACKING BOARD of some kind. I have found hardboard (Masonite) the best material and it need be no thicker than 2mm. This thin grade of hardboard has the advantage of occupying the minimum space in the rebate, which can sometimes be very shallow, and it is also easier to cut than the heavier, more commonly used types while being quite strong enough for most applications.

For fitting pictures with glass and backing board into their frames a GLAZING GUN (fig. 18) is a great help if you do much framing. This very useful device may come within the expensive luxury class of equipment for the individual but would undoubtedly earn its keep in a group workshop.

If you are making a list of your requirements from this chapter, it should include a pair of PLIERS, a SCREWDRIVER, a PUNCH (or nail-set), SCREW-EYES, HANGERS, WOOD-FILLERS, GLASS-PAPER (or sandpaper) and GUMMED TAPE (2ins or 5cm wide is ideal). I have not mentioned material for gilding because this is very specialized and must be a separate and later consideration (see chapter 7). Other details of equipment will be mentioned as their need arises but, to make a beginning, you will require most of the items mentioned here in one form or another.

There are also pieces of equipment I have not mentioned, such as G-clamps (or C-clamps), wood-planes, shooting-blocks, rasps and files, chisels, try-squares and a host of devices which I have hardly, if ever, used in spite of having made many thousands of frames for artists, collectors, stately and humble homes, and even palaces. It is all a question of method and of using that most marvellous of all equipment, the hand and eye.

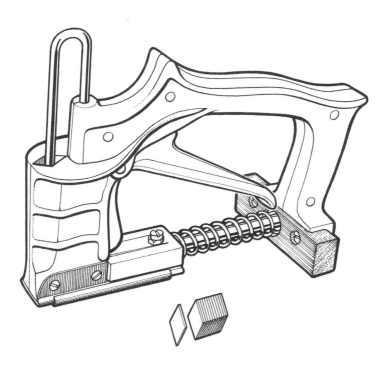

18 A glazing gun. The diamond-shaped sprigs are loaded into the magazine and shot into the rebate (rabbet) when the lever is pulled upwards.

3 Making a beginning

Choosing the frame is the most interesting yet most demanding part of the craft of framing pictures and anything that helps you to visualize the effect of one style or another is well worth setting up. The best way to begin is to make some sample corners of as many different mouldings as you can get hold of, mitred and joined to form an angle of 90°. Make them all the same size and arrange them conveniently on a panel of some kind for reference, as in the colour illustration on page 37. This will also give you some good practice in learning to join corners before starting to make a complete frame.

The following description of how to join a sample corner assumes that you have a mitre-cutter of the kind shown in fig. 13 on page 25. If you are working with a different device it should be quite easy to adapt the procedure without altering the principle of the operation.

1 Using the simple 'hockey stick' shape of moulding illustrated in fig. 9 on page 23, take 18ins (45cm) of the moulding and cut a mitre at each end (fig. 19) so that the angles form, as it were, two sides of a triangle.
2 Measuring the *back* of the moulding, make a mark exactly half-way along it and secure the moulding in the left-hand clamp of the mitre-cutter so that the mark corresponds with the centre channel at the base of the cutter (which is directly beneath the cutting edge of the saw). Then cut the mitre (fig. 20).
3 Release the moulding from the clamp and position the second half in the right-hand clamp so that a V shape is trimmed off as the last mitre is cut (fig. 21).

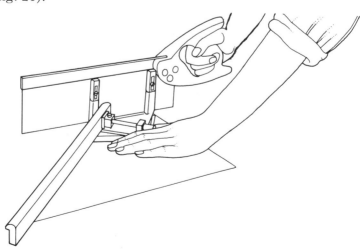

19 Cutting the first mitre from a length of moulding.

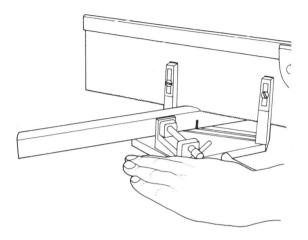

20 Cutting the mitre at the half-way mark.

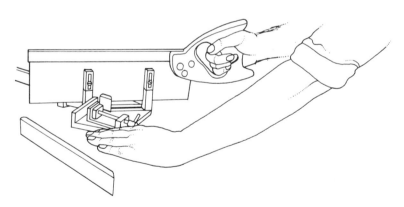

21 Cutting the last mitre for the sample corner.

The two pieces are now ready to be joined. Place them back to back and check that they are exactly the same length. One piece is gripped very firmly in the vice and the other is held in position by the *left* hand, palm upwards, leaving the right hand free to manipulate in turn the adhesive, the drill, the pins and the hammer. This may seem awkward at first, and certainly a little practice is needed, but it is a good and well-tried method of joining picture-frame mouldings and well worth the trouble you may have in getting it right.

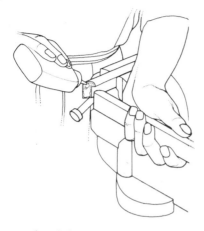

22 Applying the adhesive; one piece of moulding is gripped in the vice, the other is held in the left hand, palm upwards.

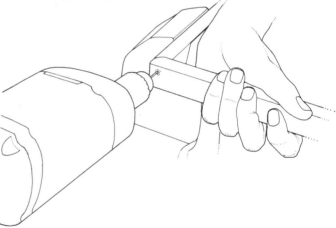

23 Drilling pilot holes for the fixing pins.

Apply the adhesive to the end of the section held in the vice, using a small brush or a squeezie bottle with a spout (fig. 22). Now bring the mitres together using only your left hand, making quite sure that they are exactly in register. With your right hand take up the electric drill (with a $\frac{1}{16}$ drill-bit in the chuck) to make the pilot holes for the two fixing pins (fig. 23). The drill-bit must go right through the section held in the left hand and pierce the section gripped in the vice. The difficult part of this operation is ensuring that the mitres are held in perfect register all the time. Now drive the pins ($\frac{3}{4} \times 18$) into the pilot holes (fig. 24) and release the left-hand hold. The pins are then counter-sunk very slightly below the surface using a punch or nail set (fig. 25) and the holes are made flush with wood-filler.

There are one or two tips worth mentioning at this stage. If you are using a mitre-cutter of the type described above, it must be firmly screwed to the bench, positioned so that the saw in its guides is at right angles to the edge of the bench. The heads of both the screw-clamps of the cutter should be padded with pieces of cardboard (pieces of mounting board will do very well) to protect the finish of the moulding. The same applies to the vice. Cut the pieces of board to the required shape and glue them in position.

Perhaps the best tip of all is – *measure twice* and *cut once*. Accurate measurement is the very essence of framing.

Having practised with some sample corners, you are now ready to frame a picture. To make a beginning, I will describe step by step the process of framing a print of Albrecht Dürer's *Hare*, originally painted in water-colour in 1502, so that it will look like the illustration in fig. 26. To give an antique feeling to the work I have chosen moulding A from page 37.

24 Driving in the pins.

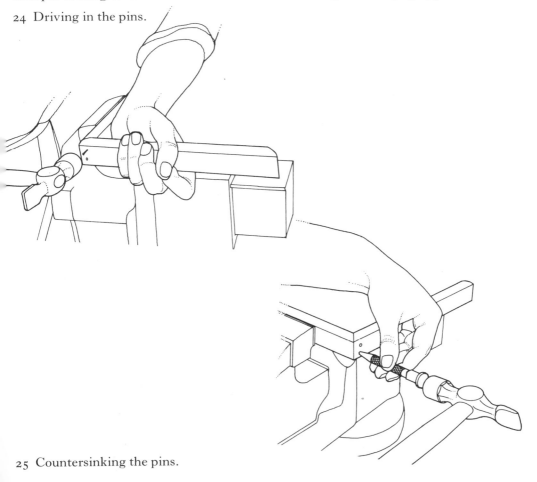

25 Countersinking the pins.

33

26 A reproduction of Dürer's *Hare*, framed in an antique style.

First the picture must be measured. Always measure height before width; this is a rule which must be followed for reasons which become important later when we want to define whether the picture is vertical or horizontal in shape. (In the USA standard measurements are made width × height; American readers should therefore be careful to follow the text directions in this respect rather than their natural inclination.) This print measures 12 × 10ins (30.5 × 25.4cm); this is called the rebate size, from which we calculate the length of moulding we shall need.

There are several methods for measuring the exact dimensions of the sides of the frame. The best system to use if you work with the type of mitre-cutter mentioned above (fig. 13) is as follows:

1 Measure the rebated edge of the moulding (see fig. 9), which in this case is 1in. (2.5cm), and add twice this dimension to the height of the picture plus $\frac{1}{16}$in. (2mm), making a total of $14\frac{1}{16}$ins (35.7cm). Again, add the 2ins (5cm) to the width of the picture plus $\frac{1}{16}$in. (2mm), which totals $12\frac{1}{16}$ins (30.6cm). These are the two measurements we need for cutting the mitres of the four sides of the frame, working from the *back* of the moulding.

2 Clamp the moulding in the cutter and cut the first mitre as described previously. Release the moulding and mark off $14\frac{1}{16}$ins (35.7cm) from the back edge of the mitre, and re-position the moulding in the other clamp so that the mark is in line with the centre channel of the cutter and directly beneath the saw, as shown in fig. 20. Cut the second mitre, thus completing the first side of the frame.

3 Another piece of moulding identical to the first is needed to form the opposite side of the frame. Again cut the first mitre. Now place the completed piece of moulding back to back with the second piece and mark off the distance for the second mitre, and follow the same sequence as above. These two pieces are the two long sides of the frame. Place them back to back again and check that they are identical.

4 The two short sides of the frame are measured and the mitres cut to the same procedure, but this time to a dimension of $12\frac{1}{16}$ins (30.6cm).

Always check both pairs of sides carefully for accuracy. If they are not perfectly identical in length, there will be gaps in the mitres when the frame is assembled and no amount of jiggery-pokery will disguise the poor workmanship and the resultant instability of the frame.

Before joining the frame you might well save some heartache later by placing the mitred sections in position upside down on the bench to see whether the picture fits; it should drop neatly into the rebate.

The sequence for joining the four mitred pieces to form the frame should be followed as a routine; in this way you will avoid such frustrating mistakes as joining the wrong two sides together.

1 Place the pair of long sides and the pair of short sides together and then take one *long* side and grip it tightly in the vice by the rebated section, leaving no more than about 3ins (7.5cm) protruding to the right of the jaws of the vice.

2 Take up a short side, holding it with the left hand palm upwards, and apply the adhesive with the right hand; carefully position the mitres together and drill two pilot holes, then hammer in the pins and counter-sink the heads, as for the sample corner (figs 22–25). Remove the joined L-shape from the vice and place it aside.

3 Take up the other long side and grip this in the vice, and join the remaining short side to it exactly as described above. Release the second joined L-shape and re-position it in the vice by its short side.

4 With the left hand holding the long side of the first L-shape, apply adhesive to *both* mitres of the L-shape now gripped in the vice. Bring the two halves together, drill the pilot holes, drive in the pins and counter-sink the heads to complete the third corner of the frame.

5 Re-position the frame once more so that the long side you have just joined is gripped in the vice, and join the last corner.

The most hazardous part of the operation is re-positioning the L-sections in the vice in order to glue and pin each pair of mitres in rotation. To make this easier, a simple prop can be constructed to support the overhanging section of moulding.

By now you will have found that some strategy is needed when drilling the pilot holes and pinning the mitres. You must be careful that the pins do not protrude from the wood and that they are spaced in the best way to pull the mitres together evenly.

Corner clamps are often advocated for joining the mitres and, to adopt the method usually recommended, a set of four are required. A number of versions are available, most of which have clamping screws to enable the mitres to be pulled up tightly after the adhesive is applied; the corners may also be pinned while thus secured. There is no doubt that this is an easier method than the one I have described and, for anyone more determined to make frames than acquire the skill of the professional, it might be the best technique to choose.

Opposite:
Some examples of 'prepared' mouldings selected from the enormous range of available patterns and made up into sample corners:

A   an antique style of ribbed moulding (fig. 26)
B   close ribbed, gilt, French style
C   Victorian 'composition' moulding (fig. 44)
D   a very useful scoop or 'spoon' shape (fig. 43)
E   box moulding with silver (aluminium) finish (fig. 41)
F   a neat modern shape with a deep back (figs 40 and 51)
G   a good traditional shape for watercolours
H   a small silver reverse shape for drawings
I   walnut finish with a gilt sight edge (fig. 33)
J   plain wood, stained and waxed (fig. 31)
K   a simple but effective gilt moulding (fig. 36)
L   the well-known 'Hogarth' moulding
M   flat gilt slip with no rebate (rabbet) (fig. 51)
N   a small angled shape with many uses (fig. 40)
O   moulding for a 'floating' frame (fig. 38)
P   deep backed capping for box frames (figs 48 and 49)
Q   plain wood slope for box frames (figs 48 and 49)
R   a good general-purpose shape for oil paintings
S   a handsome Italianate shape with a coloured 'spoon' (fig. 45)
T   a moulding with gilt and walnut finish
U   stained wood with a gilt beaded edge (fig. 28)
V   plain wood, waxed and polished
W   a canvas-covered slip with ornate gilt edge (fig. 44)
X   a wide linen-covered panel (fig. 43)
Y   a pale linen-covered slip with fluted gilt edge (fig. 41)

O

P

Q

R

S

T

U

V

W

X

Y

Now we will cut a piece of glass to fit into the rebate of the frame. In case you have skipped the preceding chapter I will repeat a cautionary word about handling glass. Do not confuse confidence with foolhardiness; it may be somebody else who gets hurt.

The working surface on which the glass is to be cut must be dead flat and free from even the smallest fragment of foreign matter. An old blanket is ideal for covering the bench to provide the small amount of cushioning necessary. The glass too must be clean or it is liable to crack unexpectedly in the wrong place while being cut. Note that the cutting point of the diamond is about $\frac{1}{16}$in. (2mm) from the side of the straight edge so adjust your cutting line accordingly. The proper way to hold the cutter is with the thumb beneath, and the index and second finger each side of the handle.

A glass-cutter's T-square is well worth adding to your equipment if you intend to do your own glass cutting. Apart from the 90° angle formed by the T at the top it is quite different from the conventional pattern: its length is calibrated and the sides are parallel so that it can be used for measuring as well as providing a straight-edge for the cutter. With the cutter firmly against the right-hand side of the straight-edge, draw it from the top edge of the glass towards you smoothly and steadily, maintaining the cutting angle the whole time. The ear is the best guide as to whether or not the operation is going successfully. A scratching noise is a certain indication of failure resulting from too much pressure; a light, gentle hissing sound is invariably the prelude to a perfect result. Now place the glass with the score mark parallel to the edge of the bench (or to the edge of the T-square) and apply pressure to the overhanging piece, causing a clean break along its length.

I would urge the beginner to practise cutting glass before attempting to glaze his first picture. A good way to get the hang of it is to take an odd piece of glass and, working from right to left, try cutting it into 1-in. (2.5cm) strips. After a while you will find the best angle (which varies greatly between one diamond cutter and another) for getting a good result. You will have achieved this when you can break off the strip by holding the piece of glass in both hands, thumbs uppermost on each side of the score mark, and snapping off the strip as if you were breaking a piece of chocolate. Do not persist if the glass does not break readily, too much force will cause a break in quite the wrong direction; try the next strip and keep trying until you get the knack of it. And if you can, watch an experienced glazier at work – this is better than any written explanation.

Glass bends, if you can believe it, and this makes it possible to employ a most useful trick of the trade when glazing a picture. The frame is placed rebate uppermost on the bench and a piece of glass is laid on top with its left-hand side in line with the left-hand rebate of the long side of the frame. A gentle downwards pressure bends the edge of the glass so that it can be lined up with great accuracy against the back edge of the rebate. Now the T-square is laid on the glass with its right-hand edge in line with the *sight edge* (see fig. 9) of the opposite side of the frame rebate, and the first side of the glass is cut. Turn both frame and glass through 90⁰ and let the left-hand short side and both long sides of the glass drop into the rebate, leaving the last piece overhanging the right-hand short side of the frame. Line up the T-square with this rebate sight edge as before and make the second and final cut, and you have a nicely fitted piece of glass – without taking any measurements. Clean and polish the glass, using equal parts of water and methylated spirit (denatured alcohol).

The backing board is cut to the same size as the glass to fit into the rebate. If your electric drill can be used with either a jig-saw or circular saw attachment, it will prove useful for this purpose.

The sequence of fitting everything together varies with different framers, but the objective must always be to seal the picture in the frame firmly, neatly and, above all, cleanly without having to take everything apart again to remove one speck of dust trapped between the picture and the glass. It is more commonly recommended that you start and finish the whole process with the frame facing downwards, but the method I prefer is to put the backing board on the bench first, place the picture on the board – having brushed them both lightly to remove any dust – and then cover it with the polished glass and place the frame in position. Inspect the picture carefully through the glass to make sure it is absolutely clean and then turn the whole assembly, including the frame, face downwards on the bench. Now secure the backing board firmly with small veneer pins tapped into the rebate with a light hammer, about 6ins (15cm) apart; to provide an effective buffer while doing this, hold a piece of 2 × 2in. (5 × 5cm) timber about 2ft (60cm) long firmly against the side of the frame. This job is easier and somewhat more elegant using the glazing gun in fig. 18, page 29.

Finally, the assembled components are sealed with 2-in. (5-cm) gummed brown paper tape, to prevent the ingress of dust from the back. Screw-eyes, or whatever hanging fitments are selected (fig. 27), are positioned one-third of the way down on each side of the frame at the back, and all is finished.

27 Hanging fitments: 'D' ring, screw ring and screw-eye.

Take a critical look at the finished job. If it is your first effort, you are likely to see something somewhere that offends your craftsman's eye or your aesthetic sensibility. Is there a tiny gap between the mitres of one corner? If you are a perfectionist you will study the reason for it and take even greater pains with your measurements next time. As for the effect upon the picture produced by the frame – this is the really intriguing question. I quite like the frame illustrated here, but wonder whether the picture might look as well if presented in another style using a traditional method of framing with a mount (mat). The next chapter describes how this is done.

4 Framing watercolours, drawings and prints

All pictures need some form of protection if they are to be preserved. Because of their particular vulnerability to the ravages of time, paintings, drawings and prints on paper in media such as watercolour, gouache, pencil, charcoal, pastel, crayon and ink have always presented a special conservation problem. With the notable exception of oil and, more recently, acrylic paintings, which are usually varnished, glass is the traditional means of surface protection. The glass must not touch the picture because of the danger of condensation, so a space, however small, must be maintained between the picture and the glass.

The cut-out, or over-lay, mount (mat) has long been the method adopted both for separating the glass from the picture and providing the many variations of shape, colour and texture associated with the framing of paintings and drawings in watercolour and the like.

As already mentioned, the choice of mounting board is very wide; but for the moment, and to pursue Dürer's hare into another form of enclosure, let us take a piece of the neutral tinted mounting board suggested in chapter 2 and follow the rather complex procedure of framing this picture so that this time the finished arrangement looks like the illustration in fig. 28.

The first decision is how much margin to allow around the picture. A nice proportion would show 3ins (7.5cm) of mount at the top and sides and 3½ins (8.8cm) at the base. The extra width at the bottom creates an optical balance without which the base appears to be narrower than it really is.

Two sets of dimensions are needed for the mount: the opening, or window, and the outside measurement which will be the rebate size for the frame. The calculation is simple enough, but remember – always height before width; if you are not consistent about this with the two sets of dimensions you will get into a nasty mess. The part of the picture we want to see, in this case, measures 12 × 10ins (30.5 × 25.4cm). We must therefore add 3ins (7.5cm) for the top and 3½ins (8.8cm) for the bottom margin to the *height* of the picture, making a total of 18½ins (46.8cm); and 3ins (7.5cm) for each side to the *width* of the picture, making a total of 16ins (40.6cm). The outside dimension of the mount – and the rebate size for the frame, when we come to it – is therefore 18½ × 16ins (46.8 × 40.6cm).

You can work on either side of the board when marking out and cutting the window of the mount, but I much prefer working on the plain side so as to keep the tinted surface unmarked and pristine throughout the operation. Start by marking out the overall size of the mount, using a pencil with a sharp point – accuracy is the watchword. Using the knife and the steel straight-edge (*not* the bevelled side), cut the board exactly along the pencilled lines.

28 Another style of frame for Dürer's *Hare*, using a mount (mat).

29 Cutting strips of mounting board with a bevelled edge, using the bevelled side of the straight-edge.

Now mark out the window of the mount as follows: first measure 3ins (7.5cm) across from the top left-hand corner and pencil a mark, then 3ins (7.5cm) across from the bottom left-hand corner. Repeat this measurement across from the top and bottom right-hand corners. Then measure 3ins (7.5cm) down the sides from both top corners, and 3½ins (8.8cm) up from both bottom corners. Join up the marks with a pencilled line and check that the opening is 12 × 10ins (30.5 × 25.4cm) exactly. There are, of course, many other ways of doing this; the important thing is to use a method that double checks the accuracy of your measurement.

It would be a simple enough matter now to cut the opening if a straight-sided cut would do, but the only elegant way to cut mounts is with a bevelled edge surrounding the picture. It takes a great deal of practice to do this well, and some experience is also needed to work the various mechanical devices described in chapter 2. Before cutting your first mount, practise the technique first by cutting bevel-edged strips from odd pieces of mounting board, using the type of knife shown in fig. 15.

Look at fig. 29. The piece of mounting board is marked out in strips 2ins (5cm) wide and laid upon another piece of board so that the tip of the blade will not be blunted when it cuts through to make the bevelled edge. Note how the left hand steadies the top of the straight-edge, keeping well out of danger should the knife slip – and that we are now working with the bevelled side of the straight-edge. The right hand grips the pad-saw handle at an angle so that the blade makes a strong, firm cut right through the board in one go. The right forearm actually rests on the flat of the straight-edge as it moves downwards, the fist and forearm forming a strong, rigid support for the knife as it cuts the bevel from top to bottom of the piece of board.

By the time you have cut a dozen or so strips in this way you should have the feel of it and be able to keep the bevel at a constant angle and the edge absolutely straight. Now try cutting some windows. A good exercise would be to take a piece of board cut to the size calculated above – $18\frac{1}{2} \times 16$ins (47×40.6cm) – and mark it out as in the diagram, fig. 30, with the outer marks corresponding to the window measurements calculated above, and then cut openings from the centre until you finish up with a mount that should do credit to our Dürer print. If you are working on the

30 Openings marked out on mounting board to practise making cut-out mounts (mats).

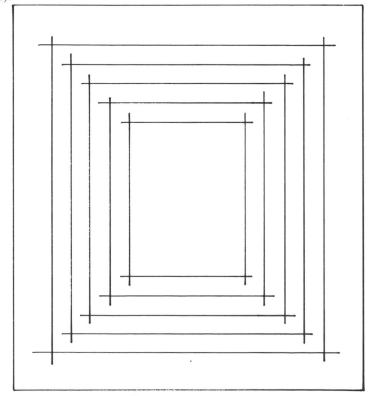

reverse side of the board, make your first cut along the line which marks the left-hand side of the window (see fig. 32, page 47). Then turn the board through 90° and cut the second side, and so on until all four sides are cut. In this way you will be sure to get the bevel sloping away from the picture surface when the board is placed right side up over the picture.

You will undoubtedly have found by now that the difficult bit is getting those beautifully bevelled corners just right. A spare sharp blade is most useful sometimes for nicking into a corner that has defied you at the last fraction of an inch; and the finest grade of garnet paper will also smooth away an irritating bit of fluffed edge that will sometimes plague the best of us.

When the mount is ready, place it over the picture and see whether or not more could be done to enhance the effect. (We will leave the choice of frame until last.) Perhaps a couple of lines in burnt sienna watercolour will give the final touch. Working now on the right (tinted) side of the mount, but making sure to keep the surface spotlessly clean, mark out the lines lightly in pencil – $\frac{3}{8}$in. (1cm) away from the bevel and $\frac{1}{8}$in. (3mm) apart. Then rule the lines with the watercolour, one thick and one thin, using a draughtsman's ruling pen if you have one or an ordinary nib. Watercolours will always flow best if diluted with distilled water, especially for the colour-washes and lines we shall come to consider later. For the present purpose the dilution should have the consistency of writing ink without being too opaque.

The print is carefully centred in the opening of the mount and a small piece of gummed paper (about 1 × $\frac{1}{2}$in. or 2.5 × 1.3cm) is used to attach the picture to the back of the mount at each of the two top corners. Do not use 'instant' or self-adhesive material for this purpose; most of these contain some form of solvent which eventually leaches through paper and can seriously mar a work of art of quality or value. It is safe if you must lick it to make it stick. It is a mistake to stick the picture to the mount in more than the two places mentioned; it must be allowed to hang within its enclosure, otherwise it may cockle (especially around the edges of the mount) after it has been framed.

Now, with mount and picture together, you can try some moulding corners to see which will look best. Modern or very elaborate shapes are not appropriate for this subject. For the frame in fig. 28 I have chosen moulding U from the samples shown on page 37. It looks neither old nor new; the simply shaped wood is stained dark and the sight edge has a running pattern of very small gilt shot. It is barely 1in. (2.5cm) in width and, after the much broader shape we tackled in chapter 3, the frame can be made with very little trouble, following the same procedure. The glass and backing board are then cut and the whole assembly completed as before.

Once you have mastered the technique of mount cutting, you will want to explore the infinite variety of decoration and embellishment that can now be employed to give breadth, richness, importance or style to pictures in this fascinating aspect of framing. So much so, indeed, that before embarking on detailed descriptions of the many possibilities afforded by the use of colour, texture, lines and washes, extra deep bevels and so on, I would urge a certain caution and restraint. Remember that it is the picture first and last that must dominate the arrangement. A gloomy picture is not going to be cheered up by a gaily coloured mount and no amount of elaborate decoration will succeed in 'tarting-up' an obviously bad piece of work. A well-designed mount is a most important factor in making the picture appear at one with its environment. Consider the picture very carefully and use your judgement to enhance it in the best way possible. This can be illustrated further by treating a series of different subjects, each with its appropriate style of mount, and using some of the various methods and ideas available.

We will start with an etching (fig. 31) made in 1928 by Orovida – the daughter of Lucien and grand-daughter of Camille Pissarro. The subject has a classical Persian flavour, depicting in the liveliest way the scarf game of its title. Two horses race across a meadow, one rider beautifully erect while the other, in the foreground, leans low out of the saddle to snatch the scarf from the ground. As in the Persian miniatures of another age, every line in the picture is immaculate and expressive, creating a total richness of tone most cleverly achieved by the etching. It is printed on a good quality hand-made paper showing a well defined plate impression; the picture area measures $10\frac{1}{2} \times 8\frac{1}{4}$ins (26.5 × 21cm). Besides the artist's signature and the date, there is also written 'State 1 – 17/20', which indicates that it was the seventeenth impression out of twenty before any alterations to the plate were subsequently made by the artist.

Perhaps the first consideration should be that the etching, by its nature, is monochromatic and we must therefore be careful that nothing in the tone or colour of the mount overbalances its delicacy. We should strive for a simple elegance of framing which takes the eye into the picture without diversion. A double mount could achieve this very well: it acts as a kind of raised step around the picture which has the effect of recessing it to the eye. A double line of warm sepia watercolour would also tone nicely with the ink of the etching; this should be $\frac{1}{2}$in. (1.3cm) from the bevelled edge of the top mount. The frame is a simple traditional 'reverse' shape (moulding J, page 37); the wood is stained dark walnut, waxed and polished.

The double mount needs to be very accurately cut to look well and the bevels of both mounts must run perfectly parallel all around the picture. The bottom mount can form a fillet of $\frac{1}{8}$–$\frac{3}{8}$in. (3–10mm) in respect of the top mount. I like to use a narrow fillet when it contrasts in colour with the top mount but allow a wider amount to show where, as in this case, both mounts are of a similar tint.

As we are now dealing with a work of art of some rarity and value, this is a good time to consider the importance of the actual material used for mounting graphic works on paper, as the mount can just as easily prove harmful to a drawing as fulfil its proper function of preserving it for many decades. Most commercial board is made from mechanical woodpulp,

31 A double mount (mat) with two lines of sepia watercolour. (Orovida *The Scarf Game*)

perhaps glazed or faced with paper. This material has many applications and is widely used and relatively cheap, but it is potentially harmful to drawings and prints of any value mainly because of its propensity for absorbing and storing acid which is present in polluted air and which subsequently affects the work in contact with it. The framer has a responsibility to posterity when handling a work of art and should ensure that the mounting board he uses is as nearly acid-free as possible. Acid-free board is much more expensive than the woodpulp boards – it is made from acid-free rag or laminated plate paper with dextrin glue – but it should be insisted upon if the work is to be cared for beyond a few years. In England this board is generally available as *mounting quality solid plate board*; in the USA it is called *conservation* or *museum mounting board* (see Suppliers, page 89).

An interesting range of tinted and textured papers are used for facing these boards (usually on one side only) and some beautiful papers with well-known names such as Ingres and Canson are associated with them. Japanese hand-made papers are also often used, and many countries produce art papers with special characteristics.

For this example I have used solid plate board faced with a pale beige tinted Italian (Fabriano) Ingres paper.

The best way to tackle cutting the double mount is like this:

1 Having cut the board for the top mount to the rebate size, cut out the window, measuring the margins as before but making them $\frac{3}{8}$in. (1cm) less to allow for the fillet formed by the bottom mount: e.g. if the overall width of the margin is to be 3ins (7.5cm) all round, then the measurement for the top mount will be 2$\frac{5}{8}$ins (6.5cm).

2 Replace the centre cut-out in the opening – the purpose of this will be seen later – leaving the mount face downwards.

3 Now cut the outside dimension of the bottom mount so that it measures 1in. (2.5cm) less than the top mount all round. Attach it to the back of the top mount by means of gummed tape (see fig. 32).

32 Making a double mount: cutting the opening of the bottom mount (mat).

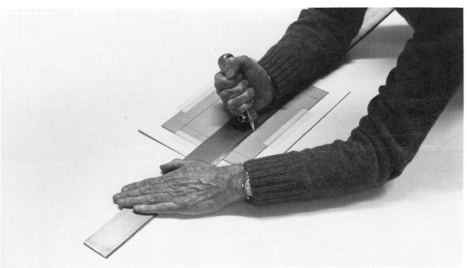

4 Mark out the opening for the bottom mount by measuring from the outer edges of the top mount. The measurements will be exactly the same as for the window of the top mount plus $\frac{3}{8}$in. (1cm). Herein lies the secret of getting both bevelled edges exactly parallel, because both openings have been measured from a single source (the outer edges of the top mount).

5 Cut the opening of the bottom mount. Because this is $\frac{3}{8}$in. (1cm) smaller all round than the window of the top mount, the tip of the blade will score the centre cut-out you replaced in the top mount as the bevel is cut.

It is helpful when attaching the bottom mount to the top mount to put a small blob or two of adhesive in the centre of the cut-out so that it cannot shift about whilst the second window is being cut. If you have made a perfect job of cutting both windows, the centres of both mounts will drop out together when the double mount assembly is turned face upwards; but you will be in good company if just the tiniest bit of niggling with a blade at one or other of the corners proves helpful.

The double mount opens the way to many methods of treating pictures that benefit from heightening the decorative effect without detracting from the interest of the subject. Fig. 33, for instance, is a delicate but

33 Another example of a double mount (mat): here a bright coloured fillet is formed by the bottom mount. (Chinese watercolour painting on rice paper).

34 A deep fillet and a fabric-covered mount (mat) are used for this pencil
drawing by Simeon Solomon.

highly coloured Chinese bird painting in watercolour on rice paper. Here,
a fillet of $\frac{1}{8}$in. (3mm) of bright green is formed by paper wrapped over the
bevel of the bottom mount, whilst the top mount is a cream tinted Canson
paper-covered board. The frame is made from moulding I on page 37.

Another form of double mount can be used to dramatize the subject in
the next example, fig. 34. This pencil drawing of Orpheus lamenting the
loss of Eurydice is by Simeon Solomon, a Pre-Raphaelite who, living in a
time far removed from present-day permissive tolerance, came to be

reviled as the dissolute and unwholesome element of the Brotherhood and died an alcoholic and a beggar. It almost seems as if the impoverished artist tried with his stub of pencil to *paint* the picture. It has an ineffably sad atmosphere. The drawing measures 18 × 15ins (45 × 38cm) and is signed and dated by the artist.

It should be treated with the importance due to a unique and original work of art, and I have tried to extend its dramatic atmosphere into the style of the frame. To achieve this I have used first a white mount with a very deep bevel (the thickness of the board is 12 sheet, twice that of the usual 6 sheet mounting board), and then a top mount covered with a finely textured charcoal grey linen which is wrapped over the bevel of the opening. The frame is in the fashion of the period, though somewhat more restrained than many of the ornate nineteenth-century plaster frames, and is gilded as described in chapter 7.

As the top mount is to be covered with a fabric which will be wrapped over the bevel, the sequence of the operation is slightly different from the preceding one:

1 First cut the outside dimension of the top mount and then the opening, replacing the centre cut-out as before.

2 Attach the piece of 12 sheet board to the top mount, and cut the opening.

3 It is now necessary to detach the top mount in order to cover it with linen. Before doing so, mark the position of the outer corners of the bottom mount on the back of the top mount, including a location mark in one corner, so that it will be a simple matter to reassemble the two mounts again.

4 A piece of the linen fabric roughly cut to size is glued to the top mount and trimmed to the outside dimensions; the wrap-over flaps are then carefully cut as shown in fig. 35 so as to form a neat finish, especially at the corners.

For covering a mount with fabric I recommend a water-soluble neoprene-based adhesive such as Unitak. This type of glue may be used either as an 'impact' adhesive, coating both surfaces to be bonded and allowing them to become almost dry before bringing them together; or by coating only the surface of the board, to which the fabric is then applied under light pressure while the emulsion dries. It may also be applied to one surface, allowed to dry off completely and then, with the fabric laid in position, re-activated by heat under pressure, forming a very good bond indeed. In the absence of a heavy dry-mounting press (see chapter 8), good results can be obtained with the practised use of a domestic electric iron.

5 The two mounts are reassembled and taped together, the picture is placed in position, and the whole assembly is fitted into the frame.

It is possible to buy 12 sheet mounting board (though you may need a little persistence to find it) but it can also be quite simply prepared by gluing two pieces of 6 sheet board together. One of the resin-based adhesives does very well for this but you must contrive some pressure over the whole area while it dries out.

Cutting the bevel through 12 sheet board calls for a strong and steady hand, some courage and a new blade every time. It looks most impressive but only when done well.

A traditional and most effective embellishment for watercolour paintings is the wash-line mount, a series of lines and a band of watercolour wash, in colours relating to the picture, on a neutral tinted mount. (In the USA this is referred to as a French mount.) In the latter part of the eighteenth century and during the nineteenth, the period which marked the height of the classical English school of watercolour painting, the works of the greatest watercolourists such as Cozens, Cox, Varley, Cotman and Turner were almost invariably framed in this style. The method continues to be used today for framing watercolours and conveys something of the aura of nineteenth-century landscape painting in the transparent watercolour washes so characteristic of the period.

35 Covering the mount (mat) with fabric wrapped over the bevel of the window. The fabric should be glued to the mount before cutting the wrap-over flaps.

To illustrate the method, I have chosen an original watercolour by H. Walcot (shown in colour opposite). It was painted around the turn of the century when both sailing vessels and steam ships shared the wharves and cranes lining the lower reaches of the River Thames. The painting exudes the atmosphere of bustling water-borne commerce and a mixture of smoke, mist and steam through which Tower Bridge dominates the background. The broad band of the river-tug's funnel markings provides the artist with a fortuitous splodge of brilliant red. A three-masted schooner lies gracefully at anchor, and the white seagulls contrast with the dark painted bollards rising strongly out of the murky, viridian-tinged water – all providing ideas for the wash-line mount.

A smooth surface is required for wash-lines, so I have chosen a Canson paper-faced board, very slighted tinted, for the mount, using margins of $3\frac{1}{2}$ins (8.8cm) with 4ins (10.2cm) at the base. The opening for the picture is $8 \times 12\frac{1}{2}$ins (20.3 × 31.8cm), so the outside measurements for the mount and the frame rebate will be 15 × 20ins (38.1 × 50.8cm). Having cut the window, the arrangement of the lines and wash can now be planned. Guide-lines are first lightly pencilled around the opening, starting with the first one $\frac{3}{8}$in. (1cm) from the bevel. Next is a pair of lines for the band of colour-wash, $\frac{1}{2}$in. (1.3cm) apart and $\frac{1}{8}$in. (3mm) away from the first line; and finally a double line $\frac{1}{4}$in. (6mm) away from the last line. I deplore the method, often advocated, of pricking into the board to mark out the lines, as it produces unsightly miniature pools of colour when the wash is applied.

The band of colour-wash is applied first. You need a soft bristle flat $\frac{1}{2}$-in. (1.3-cm) brush for this. For this painting I have chosen a watery green wash mixed in two strengths from a tube of viridian watercolour; one will be for the band of colour-wash, the other for outlining it in the same colour but of greater density. The colour-wash is pure (distilled) water with two or three drops of the stronger solution added so as to impart a greenish tinge to the water and no more. Using a full brush, several layers of the wash are applied between the pair of guide-lines until a subtle, even and transparent hint of colour is obtained. This must be quite dry before the next move, which is to colour the line nearest the opening. You really need a ruling pen for this work so that the coloured lines can be of different thicknesses. For the first line we can be quite bold and echo the only crimson blob in the picture, on the funnel of the tug. This line is relatively thin, about half a millimetre, and the colour should not be too solid. Next, the band of colour-wash is outlined with the stronger viridian solution using a thicker line, almost a millimetre, and ruling the inner line first, then the outer. For the final double line I have used burnt umber, ruling one thin and one thicker line about $\frac{1}{16}$in. (2mm) apart.

When you have made a success of a wash-line mount it is very satisfying to study its effect upon the picture (though most disheartening if you find your colouring too brash or discordant). Examine the effect under glass, because if you look carefully enough you will see that the glass imparts its

A wash-line mount. (H. Walcot: *The Pool of London*)

36 A gold band flanked by fine watercolour lines enhances this 19th-century
watercolour landscape.

own very faint green tinge, almost indiscernible but enough, in this case, to
enhance very slightly the green colour-wash. With a gold leaf frame of
simple but elegant shape, the final effect is traditional and very pleasing.

Fig. 36 is a small watercolour landscape, not by a great master of the
technique but none the less charming. A friend gave it to me in exchange
for framing half-a-dozen by the same artist which he had bought for a very
small sum. The illustration shows a good way to frame such pictures
economically yet impeccably. The mount is a very pale tinted Ingres
paper-faced board, with a ⅛in. (3mm) band of gummed gold paper laid ⅜in.
(1cm) away from the opening, and flanked by lines of raw umber watercolour. The frame is made from moulding K on page 37. Guide-lines for
the band of gold paper can be pencilled in and will serve as the basis for the
flanking lines of watercolour.

Gold paper gummed on one side is most useful for decorating mounts.
It can be cut into various widths for applications such as the one just
described or used for covering the bevel of the mount opening as in fig. 37.

37 The circular opening for this small 19th-century sketch by Lord Leighton
of Stretton is covered with a strip of gummed gold paper; the mount (mat) is
covered with pink shot silk.

It is also effective as a gold fillet with double mounts. A trick with this paper is to flick a dark spirit stain onto it by rubbing your fingertip over the stain-moistened bristles of a toothbrush before cutting the strips, to produce an antique gold effect. Gold ink may also be used for lining mounts, but it needs more careful handling than watercolour as it does not flow freely. I find the self-adhesive metallic gold strip sometimes used is too shiny and mechanical for anything other than commercial art-work.

Oval or circular mounts are sometimes required for particular drawings, especially for vignettes where the picture is shaded off into a circle or oval. It is so difficult to cut a bevelled oval or circle free-hand with any degree of precision that I whole-heartedly recommend the special devices produced for this purpose. They are, however, far too expensive for the amateur to contemplate, and I suggest therefore that you get a professional mount-cutter to make these special mounts for you. For circular openings the only dimension required is the diameter, but as there are so many variants of the oval, from thinly eliptical to almost circular, the shape must be expressed by the dimensions of the vertical and horizontal planes of a cross.

A modern piece of needlework with an old-fashioned charm, framed as described on page 72. (Embroidery by Christopher Clarke)

5 *Framing oil paintings*

For centuries the most widely used material on which artists have painted in tempera and oil has been canvas or some similar fabric, usually supported by an adjustable frame called a stretcher. This is made so that the corners, which slot into each other, may be forced open by wedges, or keys, thus holding the fabric taut once it has been fastened to the stretcher.

Oil paintings are also frequently seen on wooden panels, sometimes of great age, and here the most careful handling is required because of the dangers arising from warping, cracking, and even splitting, of the dried wood.

Today, many artists paint on to prepared panels of compressed wood-fibre which, due to the inert nature of the bonding medium used, may prove less subject to the disintegrating effects of time than natural materials. In spite of this, canvas is still the choice of most painters in oils, who rightly question the merits of modern technology where painting is concerned, when only posterity can show whether synthetic resins and compressed fibre will support oil paintings as effectively as the materials which have carried the works of the great masters over the centuries. Acrylic paint, which is also increasingly used now, is subject to the same uncertainty. I wonder what Leonardo, that greatest of innovators, would have used had he had the choice.

The framer is rarely called upon to construct a stretcher. It is certainly simpler to go to the specialist supplier for this. To make a stretcher in the manner of a frame with rigidly joined mitred corners is to court trouble; when, inevitably, the canvas slackens it cannot be made taut without totally dismantling both frame and canvas.

Measuring an oil painting for its frame often requires calculating the *sight* size instead of the rebate sizes we have considered so far. This is because the canvas frequently forms varying areas of thickness, especially at the corners where it is wrapped over and attached to the stretcher, thereby making accurate measurement doubtful. Oil paintings, whether on canvas or panels, are also notoriously out of square and it is always important to measure both ends of the height and width of the picture. The sight size is what you will actually see of the picture when it is framed. Calculating the sight size of a painting not only takes care of small dimensional discrepancies but also ensures that when the composition extends to the very edges of the canvas or panel the minimal amount of picture is hidden in the rebate.

When measuring the moulding for framing a picture measured as a sight size, your calculations must be based on the *sight edge* of the moulding instead of its rebate (see fig. 9, page 23).

Many oil paintings are, for a variety of reasons, so grossly out of square that special difficulties arise for the framer – to put it mildly. In my

58

experience, the artist who is most obsessive about showing the very edges of his painting is the one whose canvas or panel needs most attention before it can be properly framed. He cannot bear the thought that something of his painting needs to be sacrificed in the mundane interests of right-angled corners. With what I imagined was gentle cynicism, I once proposed a rhomboidal frame, and to my horror the notion was greeted with instant enthusiasm!

If you are dealing with an important work of art, re-stretching the canvas or trimming a panel may require the attention of an expert, or, if the work is contemporary, a suitable rapport with the artist. In such matters the alliance between the artist and framer can sometimes be an uneasy one.

Where it is essential to show the very edge of the painting, it is best to pin flat wooden beading, the same thickness as the depth of the frame rebate, to the edge of the stretcher and frame onto that; but first see that all corners are true right-angles.

Oil paintings are peculiarly susceptible to inappropriate framing; visual judgement and a careful assessment of the picture are quite as important as the craftsmanship required to make the frame. There are many matters to consider in choosing the best frame for a particular oil painting; style, period, cost, the artist's particular view, the trend of fashion and the place where the picture will live are just some factors which affect the result. But, above all else, I have come to believe that the magic word is *atmosphere*, by which I mean that when the ambience of the painting is enhanced by its presentation, it sings out of the frame. It is then that, as Degas is said to have commented, 'the frame is the reward of the artist'.

A great deal could be said and debated on this point, but the importance of understanding as much as possible about the painting, and indeed the painter, is certain. However, as example is better than precept, let us take a few samples from the infinite range of paintings that might come within our sphere of interest and consider a possible approach for each picture.

The first is an oil painting on canvas, measuring 40 × 32ins (101.6 × 81.3cm), (fig. 38). The subject, a young lady of ten years old, is obviously much at home in the artist's studio; her bright demeanor, which I know well from many drawings and studies by this artist, is what creates the atmosphere of the work. Quite apart from the harsh economics of the artist's vocation, framing this style of painting demands great simplicity, and nothing could be more simple in both design and construction than the following procedure.

The moulding used here is made up from two lengths of timber $1\frac{7}{8}$ × $\frac{1}{2}$in. (4.8 × 1.3cm) and $1\frac{1}{8}$ × $\frac{3}{8}$in. (2.9 × 1cm) in cross section. For this frame, two 7-ft (220cm) lengths of each size will be enough and to spare. The two sizes are glued and pinned together as shown in fig. 39a, using resin-based adhesive and 1-in (25-mm) veneer pins about 6ins (15cm) apart. There is no need to countersink the pins as they will not be seen. The simple moulding thus formed is mitred and joined in the usual way. Measurements must be carefully calculated to ensure that the canvas is a

38 This picture appears to float in its frame owing to the shadow formed by the recessed, black-painted area between the painting and the top edge of the frame. (David Remfry: *Tamara*)

snug fit within the frame; the step formed by the moulding is *not* the rebate; in this case there is no rebate and a special method for securing the picture to the frame will be used.

The frame is now given a smooth finish with garnet paper, paying particular attention to the top edge (see diagram below), and then a coat of wood primer. When this is dry, a black undercoat is applied over the primer, and then a matt black finishing paint is painted on all but the top edge. The top edge only is painted green, as close as possible in tone to the green of the plant in the picture, using emulsion paint tinted with gouache colour, and is then given a satin-like sheen by burnishing with fine wire wool, and waxed and polished. The frame is now ready to be fitted to the canvas.

We want to position the canvas within the frame so that the picture surface is about $\frac{1}{8}$in. (3mm) below the frame's top edge. To do this, a piece of fibre-board or similar material $\frac{1}{8}$in. (3mm) thick is cut to the size of the picture and covered with protective fabric so that the painted surface of the picture is safe from any damage when placed upside down on it on the bench. The frame is now placed over the back of the picture so that the top edge is resting on the bench and the surface of the picture is $\frac{1}{8}$in. (3mm) higher than this.

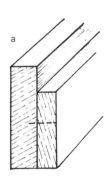
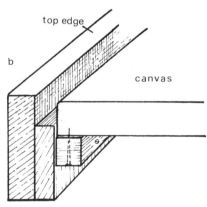

39 Making a floating frame: **a** the two pieces of timber are glued and pinned together; **b** battens are screwed first to the inside edge of the frame and then to the underside of the stretcher to secure the picture in the frame.

The picture is secured to the frame by means of four pieces of wood fixed to the inside edge of the frame at the back. These battens should be $\frac{1}{2}$in. (1.3cm) square in cross section and about 24ins (60cm) long. Make two pairs of clearance holes for screws in each batten, at 90° to each other, so that they can be screwed first to the inside edges of each side of the frame and then, very carefully, to the corresponding sections of the stretcher at the back of the canvas (fig. 39b). For $\frac{1}{2}$-in. (1.3cm) square battens, screws no longer than $\frac{5}{8}$in. (1.6cm) are perfectly adequate – it is better to be safe than sorry. It would be a mistake to screw the battens to the stretcher first, because it would then be difficult to attach them to the frame without damaging the canvas while manipulating the screwdriver.

Carefully seal the back with gummed paper strip, folding and trimming as you proceed so as to make a neat finish (the backs of picture frames should always be as neat and tidy as the front). Because this picture is not sitting in a rebate, it is quite possible to see daylight through cracks between the edge of the stretcher and the inside edge of the frame, and the sealing strip prevents this and is therefore particularly important. To enhance the shadow or moat effect produced by this kind of framing, I find that binding the edge of the stretcher with $\frac{1}{2}$-in. (1.3-cm) black tape is neat and effective. The edge of the tape should, however, be at least $\frac{1}{16}$in. (2mm) back from the surface plane of the picture.

This style of frame is particularly effective with many kinds of modern paintings, including abstracts. The shadow formed between the painting and the top edge of the frame makes the painting appear to float in its frame. The coloured top edge gives the frame great versatility. With the rest of the construction matt black, the top edge can be given a silver finish, perhaps for pictures with blue or cold tones, or gilt for a richer effect; stained and polished wood finishes can work well with many paintings, and colour, from the palest lilac wash to a solid glossy vermilion, provides a very wide choice. The proportions used here work well for a wide range of picture sizes. (Moulding O on page 37 is made up exactly as described above.)

Framing very small oil paintings presents a special challenge because the picture can so easily be swamped by the wrong kind of frame. Fig. 40 shows an example of a tiny painting on a panel measuring $7 \times 3\frac{1}{4}$ins (18×8.3cm). It shows the cosy welcome of the cottage kitchen enjoyed by the artist after a walk in the hills in early spring. The smallness of the painting is part of the intimacy of the scene; a well-worn dressing gown over a chair, wild primroses in a jar, the brown earthenware teapot, bread and a pot of jam and much more all find space within this tiny format of a few square inches.

The picture is too small to allow even a fraction to be obscured by the rebate, so first a simple gilt beaded surround is made from a small angled moulding with no rebate (sample N, page 37) into which the picture is secured by a small blob of glue in each corner. The angled base of the beading is in turn glued onto a fibre-board base covered with a beige linen

40 A tiny oil painting, $7 \times 3\frac{1}{4}$ins (18×8.3cm), framed so as to give it maximum breathing space. (Charlotte Ardizzone: *The Cottage Kitchen*)

A water-gilded frame, described opposite, designed to give breadth and richness to a small oil painting. (Diana Armfield: *Autumn Flowers from a Welsh Mountain Garden*)

material, showing a margin of 2ins (5cm) all round; this is capped by a frame made from moulding sample F. In this way the little painting is given some breathing space and retains its simple charm.

A variation of this idea for a somewhat larger painting (fig. 41) by the same artist, where we can afford to take a fraction into the rebate, uses a prepared linen-covered slip with a fluted gilt edge (sample Y) and then a simple box moulding. Although it is not necessary for an oil painting, glass is used here between the slip and the frame rebate; it can add a rather precious quality to a small painting, especially of the kind often described as sensitive.

Glass is frequently used with oil paintings to provide a protective barrier but there are also times when it can positively enhance a small delicate work and it should never be regarded as completely inappropriate for *all* oil paintings. The picture surface must not touch the glass; it can be separated by a slip, of which there are many shapes and sizes, or by an 'invisible slip' which is simply some kind of beading no wider than the frame's rebate. A useful general-purpose size for making invisible slips is $\frac{1}{4} \times \frac{3}{16}$in. (6 × 10mm) in cross section; a dark stain along the one exposed edge that might be noticed is the only finish required.

Slips and panels of many kinds are widely used in the framing of oil paintings. Quite apart from the practical aspect, when glass is used, of keeping the painted surface away from the glass, their greatest advantage is in providing a transition from the painting to the frame. To this end they can be narrow or very wide, flat, gently or steeply sloping, stained, coloured or covered with fabric or veneers. Most of these shapes are provided with a rebate in the same way as ordinary frame mouldings. In general terms, a slip is a simple moulding usually narrower than the frame proper, while a panel is almost always considerably wider than the outer frame.

When two (or more) different mouldings are used to make a frame, each is made up in the normal way, measuring the inner one to fit the picture and calculating the rebate size of the outer component to fit the outside dimensions of the slip or panel.

For the flower painting opposite I have used three components, as well as glass which I decided would enhance this work. I have tried to find the best means of sustaining the magic that has captured the volatile light and the constant movement of the flowers in the charming Victorian tea cup and converted them into this small still life; although when we were dicussing the work, the artist commented that flowers are by no means 'still life', and in this case I am bound to agree.

The first component in the design of this frame is a small flat slip about $\frac{3}{8}$in. (1cm) wide which is covered with a very pale green, fine-textured linen. This separates the picture from the glass and both glass and slip are held in the rebate of the panel which forms the second component. The panel is $1\frac{1}{2}$ins (3.8cm) wide and has a slightly raised milled sight edge which is gilded; the rest of the panel has a green tinted watercolour wash on a gesso base and is waxed. The final outer moulding is also gilded.

41 A frame combining a linen-covered slip with fluted gilt edge, and a
simple box moulding. (Charlotte Ardizzone: *Tuscany Landscape*)

42 A panel painted to tone with the picture, a water-gilded sight edge and a
reeded outer moulding. (Ethel Walker: *Portrait of a Young Girl*)

While such a frame is designed to give richness and breadth to a small
painting, it can occasionally be used with marvellous effect on a much
larger scale as, for instance, in fig. 42. This kind of framing, however,
embodies skills of construction, colouring and gilding which may well be
beyond the scope of the amateur and certainly the beginner; but the
general design can be followed by anybody, and a good approximation of
the same effect can be achieved with quite simple facilities. Indeed, the

43 A 'spoon'-shaped moulding combined with a wide linen-covered
    panel. (Ken Howard: *Cornish Beach Scene*)

44 A period style of moulding generally available, combined with a canvas-covered slip with ornate gilt edge provides an appropriate setting for this 19th-century portrait by Frederick Smallfield.

permutations that can be worked out with one or two slips and panels and a small range of mouldings – plus a dash of ingenuity – are endless, and experiment will prove interesting and rewarding. Two more examples are shown in figs 43 and 44.

I find framing oil paintings the most demanding aspect of picture framing, although it is difficult to say why this should be so. Perhaps an oil painting is in some way more intensely individualistic than other forms of visual art; whatever the reason, each one is a unique and challenging framing problem. It often happens that nothing seems to be quite right for a particular work until, suddenly, you find the way to do it and know at once that nothing else could do as well. The best practical help in assessing what works well and lends expression to your creative ideas is a range, however modest, of sample corners of mouldings.

45 A modern oil painting framed with a wide 'reverse' moulding which has a dark green painted 'spoon' between the two moulded sections. (Michael Blaker: *Nude with Cat*)

6 Framing objects, fabrics
and other materials

Once your skill as a picture framer is established among your friends and
relations, your help is bound to be sought and appreciated for framing a
wide variety of objects and materials. Photographs, mirrors, collage and
needlework, butterflies, stamps, coins and medals, parchment and vellum,
fans and fossils are but some that are certain to come your way. All are
interesting framing problems, where ideas and ingenuity will provide
rewarding solutions.

For photographs, the problem is more to do with making a 'strut-back'
for standing on the sideboard or piano than anything else. If the photograph is to be framed for hanging on the wall, nothing need be said here
that is not included in earlier chapters; but the free-standing frame should
be treated rather differently. If you use a cut-out mount, its margins
should be much narrower for a free-standing picture than a hanging one, if
only for reasons of space, and the moulding for the frame should be as light
as possible and in the same proportion.

The strut-back hinge shown in fig. 46 is a most useful device for free-
standing frames, designed to open to the required angle for the strut and
no more. It is attached first to the strut and then to the backboard of the
frame by means of bifurcated rivets, which are very easy to use. You
simply pierce holes in the board with the bradawl, push the rivets through
the hinge and the board, and hammer the two wings (bifurcations) of the
rivet flat.

46 A useful hinge for making
    a strut-back frame.

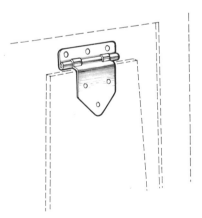

A good way to make a strut is from a stout piece of fibre-board in the form
of an isosceles triangle, 4ins (10cm) at the base and about 10ins (25cm)
high. If you make a small stock of these you can cut off the top and bottom
to suit the particular job in hand. An elegant finish is provided by covering
the board with fabric.

Once you can make frames, you can also produce mirrors in great variety, made to measure for any and every part of the house. Make the frame to the size you want, using the moulding of your fancy; order the mirror glass cut to size, with a $\frac{3}{4}$-inch (2cm) bevel if you can afford it, from a glass specialist. If the mirror glass is not bevelled around the edges, paint the inside of the rebate black to offset the reflection of plain wood you would otherwise see. Renovated old frames, though rarely the right size or type to suit a painting you want to frame, are very suitable for mirrors, and are most effective in surroundings containing antique furniture.

Embroidery and needlecraft of many kinds can be framed to great advantage and, quite apart from its decorative value, framing is the best way to preserve such work. It is best, as a rule, to stretch the work onto fibreboard before measuring for the frame; until this is done and the work accurately squared up, you cannot be sure about the dimensions for framing.

There are a dozen different ways of stretching needlework, but, for most applications, an ordinary stapling machine is the best device, provided of course that there is a small margin of spare material around the edge of the work, as is usually the case. In the illustration on page 57, the stitchery forms a circular composition and the hessian (burlap) base is held between two wooden rings, the outer one being adjustable so that the work can be kept tightly stretched. The work could, of course, be removed from its stretcher and laid onto a base before framing. However, in this case the stretcher has been retained and fitted into a circular frame after chiselling out a clearance in the rebate for the adjusting screw. This allows the work to be removed easily from the frame and re-tensioned if and when it should become necessary – just as with the stretcher of an oil painting. Glass is necessary for the protection of framed embroidery but it is important to avoid surface contact, so a separating slip of some kind must be used. In this case the outer, adjustable ring of the embroidery support is positioned slightly above the surface of the stitchery before tightening the screw, so that a separate slip becomes unnecessary (fig. 47).

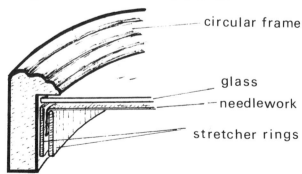

circular frame

glass

needlework

stretcher rings

47 Cross-section showing how the outer ring of the embroidery stretcher is positioned slightly higher than the inner ring to support the glass clear of the stitchery (see colour illustration, page 57).

Labels within the frame:

G.C.B.
(military)

Order of Merit
(military)

China 1857   Crimea 1854-6   Baltic 1854-5   Jubilee 1897   Coronation 1902   Crimea (Turkish)   Military Valour (Italian)

Order of the Medjidie
(Turkish)

Légion d'Honneur
(French)

ORDERS & MEDALS OF
ADMIRAL OF THE FLEET, THE HON: SIR H. KEPPEL, G.C.B, O.M.
BORN, JUNE 14TH 1809, DIED, JAN: 17TH 1904.

48 Decorations and insignia displayed in a box frame.

Needlecraft remains particularly (but by no means entirely) a ladies' province, and their help and advice in matters affecting trimming, cleaning, ironing, stretching etc. can be most important in the successful framing of this kind of work.

Framing coins and medals involves the special fascination of working towards the best lay-out of the items that are to be framed. Imagine a box full of assorted medals and insignia from which the illustrious presentation in fig. 48 was obtained, and you will see what I mean.

Velvets in rich deep blues or reds are indicated here, to cover both the base and the steep sloping slip which acts as the 'spacer' supporting the glass against the rebate of the frame and also provides the rebate for the base. Before the velvet is laid onto the base the lay-out is worked out and holes are drilled in the board with circle-cutters to the diameter of the medals. This is a tricky business as each medal must be a tight push-fit *after* the velvet has been laid (see page 50 for covering board with fabric); it is best to do some trial runs with a piece of board and some odd bits of velvet before embarking on the final design. Cross-slits are then made in the velvet where each hole has been cut and transparent nylon thread is used for securing the ribbons and any other insignia which, because of their shape, must be fastened to the surface of the velvet.

This kind of box frame, using a moulding with a very deep back such as samples P and Q, page 37, is the best assembly for the display of three-dimensional objects of all kinds, from antique fans to rare butterflies, and imparts a museum-like aura to whatever it encloses. The only special feature of construction is that both the 'capping' (the moulding with the deep back) and the 'slope' must have a rebate, one to accommodate the glass, the other for securing the base (fig. 49).

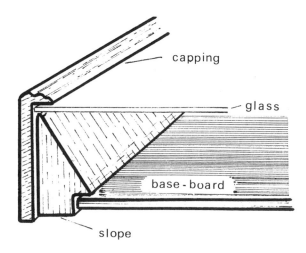

49 Cross-section of a box frame.

50 The two mounts for drawings
on either side of the same sheet
of paper to be framed in a
double-sided frame. (Drawings
by Bernard Dunstan)

The phrase 'seeing the other side of the coin' frequently applies to framing. Not only coins and medals, but documents, prints and drawings often have something of special interest on the reverse side to warrant either a window or, in the case of two drawings of equal interest occupying both sides of the paper, glass over the entire area of each surface.

Where a window is required to show, perhaps, a small preparatory sketch or an important signature, it can be cut out of the backing board and, providing only a small area is involved, a piece of transparent acetate sheet of fairly stout gauge (or several thin layers) taped to the *inside* of the opening in the backboard is usually quite adequate for both display and protection. However, where the whole area of both surfaces is to be seen, what is required is virtually a double frame.

As an example of making a double-sided frame, I have chosen two small sketches of a child's head, one on each side of a small piece of paper, by Bernard Dunstan. Both are equally delightful and each merits the same attention.

First make a suitable cut-out mount for each drawing; the openings will differ but both must have the same outside dimensions (fig. 50). Now select a moulding with a rather deeper rebate than usual for the main frame

51 One side of the double frame on its wooden base.

(e.g. sample F, page 37); ideally it should accommodate two thicknesses of glass and the two cut-out mounts. When the frame has been joined and the two pieces of glass are cut to size, the first piece of glass is put into the frame rebate followed by the drawings sandwiched between the two cut-out mounts, then the second piece of glass. Now, using the small gilt slip without a rebate (sample M, page 37), cut the mitres so that the *outer* edge of the gilt slip registers with the outside edge of the reverse side of the frame. Using the minimum number of brass veneer pins (about six should do), secure the gilt slip to the rebated edge of the frame to hold the whole assembly together.

All this depends, of course, on the top piece of glass being more or less flush with the rebated edge of the frame. If you cannot achieve this it is much better to have a rebate that is too deep rather than too shallow and use a slip or some other device to secure the assembly inside the rebate. This may not look as neatly finished as the former method, but paint or thin strips of adhesive black tape or passe-partout can be used for tidying up where necessary.

With a double picture of this sort it is a pity to mar one side with screw-eyes and picture wire for wall hanging, which almost certainly ensures that only one side will ever be seen, so the answer is to mount the picture on a simple wooden base (fig. 51). Clearance holes should be made in the base for screwing it to the bottom of the frame moulding, taking care to use screws of the correct length to ensure they stop well short of where the glass rests in the frame rebate. Green baize should be glued to the base to protect furniture surfaces.

7 Gilding

In spite of changes of taste and style, gilding has always been and still remains the decorative finish *par excellence* for picture frames. Although the term is frequently used to embrace many kinds of decoration which simulate gold, gilding in its true sense is the art of covering a surface with thin gold leaf, thus producing the effect of solid metal.

There is ample evidence that gilding was practised thousands of years ago by the ancient Egyptians and the Chinese; it is mentioned in the Old Testament of the Bible and referred to in Greek literature. The extraordinary malleability of gold has enabled this legendary and proverbial metal to be hammered into thinner and thinner sheets as techniques improved through the centuries. At the time of the ancient Romans, Pliny the Elder described how a single ounce of gold could be beaten into 750 thin leaves 'measuring four fingers each way'. Today, the same ounce of gold provides about 2,000 leaves (assuming Pliny's four fingers measured 3ins or 7.5cm in width) and would cover an area of about 100 sq. ft (10 sq. m). Standard leaf, which is $23\frac{1}{2}$ carat gold is, incredibly, 1/300,000th of an inch thick. It is available in books of leaves, 3ins (7.5cm) square, packed between tissue, usually twenty leaves to a book.

The use of gold in the form of applied leaf for the framing of works of art is certainly part of the universal history of man's desire for what is most precious and permanent as a decorative substance. For thousands of years the rarity and natural beauty of gold has maintained its constant appeal. It does not glitter, as the proverb implies, but shines with a steady natural lustre; it does not tarnish and is virtually impervious to age and decay. All this, together with its beauty of colour and texture and its unique ductility, has evoked the highest and most delicate forms of craftsmanship for thousands of years.

The oldest and by far the pre-eminent form of gilding in fine-art picture framing is called *water-gilding*, in which the leaf is laid onto a ground consisting of several coats of gesso and bole and then burnished with an agate stone to a bright sheen. No picture framer who aspires to the epitome of his craft can really frame the loveliest works without recourse to water-gilding. The method is described here, but it is an art which can only be acquired by long and painstaking practice following and observing the technique of a master gilder or attending one of the special courses available.

The preparation of the frame for water-gilding is of paramount importance. Gesso – pronounced 'jesso', Italian for chalk – is a white fluid made up from whiting (precipitated chalk) mixed with rabbitskin or, sometimes, parchment glue to a consistency in which the glue solution controls the degree of hardness required by the gilder. Two grades of gesso are used:

hard, or coarse, which is plain gypsum or plaster of Paris, and soft, the finest grade of whiting.

The container of gesso is heated in a glue pot or double boiler to prevent the solution from boiling and forming lumps or being allowed to cool and set into a jelly. Several coats are applied with a brush to the wood surface of the frame, and then sandpapered to a smooth finish; usually two coats of hard and four coats of soft gesso are used. As the gesso is applied it has the appearance and opacity of very thin cream.

Bole, variously called French clay, Armenian bole or poliment, is applied over the gesso. Bole is a soft clay of a somewhat oily texture containing iron oxide; it is commonly red, but black, yellow, brown and blue boles are also used to create certain effects when the burnished gold leaf is 'distressed', as described later.

The bole is made up into a smooth creamy mixture containing parchment or gelatine so that it acts both as ground and gold-size for the leaf. Up to four coats of bole are applied and rubbed down with glass paper to provide a velvety, flawless and absorbent surface ideal for water-gilding.

A gilder's cushion, a gilder's knife and a gilder's tip are required for applying the leaf to the bole ground (fig. 52).

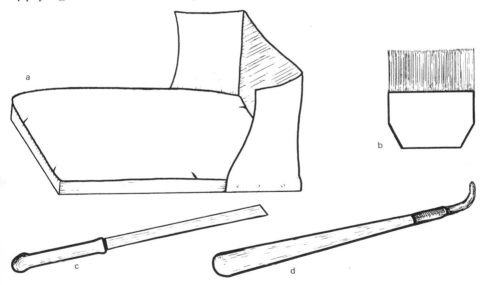

52 **a** Gilder's cushion   **b** Gilder's tip   **c** Gilder's knife   **d** Gilder's burnisher

The cushion is a padded, suede-covered board with a thumb grip for supporting it and a sheath for the knife. It measures about 6 × 12ins (15 × 30cm) and has a draught screen of stiff Kraft paper enclosing about a third of the board; the smallest draught is enough to send the precious leaves sailing through the air to finish up a tiny worthless heap on the floor.

The knife is used for dividing the leaves into the required segments for laying onto the surface of the ground. It is manipulated with a sawing motion to cut the leaf, but the edge is not so sharp that it can damage the suede pad.

The gilder's tip is a thin, wide brush rather sparsely equipped with camel hair and is used for picking up the leaf. Water, containing a small amount of gelatine and sometimes methylated spirit (denatured alcohol) is applied to the bole surface with a soft mop brush immediately before the leaf is laid. With the cushion held in his left hand, the gilder strokes his beard or his hair with the tip in order to make it very slightly oily so that the fragile leaf clings to the tip until it is laid onto the moistened surface of the bole to which it firmly adheres.

The burnisher (fig. 52d) is the instrument used for creating the smooth high gloss characteristic of water-gilding. Various shapes and sizes of polished agate mounted in wooden handles are used in this technique. Before starting to burnish, the gilder taps the leafed surface to ensure the work is sufficiently dry, which is indicated by a ringing tone. If it is not, the leaf will be ripped by the stone and the surface spoilt.

In the process of burnishing, the malleable leaf is smoothed and pressed into the bole until a lustrous finish is obtained; much experience is required before a perfect burnished finish can be achieved, particularly when the frame moulding has an entirely smooth surface where scratch marks can result from unskilled or over-hasty burnishing. Where the moulding has some carving or ornamentation or is reeded, burnishing is obviously limited to the higher parts of the pattern and a mat finish is retained in those areas which the burnisher cannot reach, creating an effect of richness and contrast.

Brightly burnished gilded frames are, however, the exception rather than the rule for modern works of art. Most artists and collectors like to see the gold toned or distressed. The Renaissance gilders frequently toned the flat panel section of the frame with dull tempera colour over the gold, and the same technique is employed today, although watercolour washes and sometimes thin oil colours are used rather than tempera. The effect of toning is best when applied to a part of the frame such as the spoon, or concavity, of the moulding or, as previously mentioned, the panel.

Distressing is quite different to toning. It implies the removal of some of the gold that has been so laboriously laid and burnished, to the point where the colour of the bole begins to show through in greater or lesser degree, leaving a recurring pattern of thin bands of deeper gold where the gold leaf has been overlapped slightly when laid and is thus twice the thickness of the rest of the gilding. In this technique, the colour of the bole plays an important part in the final effect. Black bole showing through a distressed gold finish can be quite opulent and dramatic; brown will be rich and warm, a red even warmer (it is akin to Indian or Venetian red), and yellow relatively cool and metallic. A little black mixed with the commonly available natural red bole is my own preference, but the subtleties of distressed gilding are very much a matter of personal choice and taste and, as always, what best suits the painting should be the criterion.

Methods for distressing the burnished leaf vary, but the experienced gilder often uses a pad of cotton wool containing soft beeswax and, with a light and careful touch, smoothes the surface until just the right degree of colour is achieved.

Moisture of any kind is the arch-enemy of a water-gilded surface – many a disaster has followed the enthusiastic use of a damp duster vigorously applied to a water-gilded frame. The surface could be protected by a lacquer, but this is never (or *should* never) be used on a water-gilded finish because rather like non-reflective glass on a delicate watercolour drawing, it creates a plastic effect and the natural lustre is lost. If kept dry, the water-gilded frame retains its beauty for hundreds of years.

Silver leaf is quite frequently used and is applied by the same technique as gold but, because silver tarnishes so readily, white-gold leaf (which is roughly equal parts of silver and 12 carat gold) is the most widely used material. This also tarnishes to some degree and requires a protective lacquer if it is to retain its sheen. None of the silver finishes, however, have the intrinsic beauty of water-laid gold leaf, although silver can be very effective for certain paintings, especially where cool tones predominate.

A mat finish may be obtained by omitting the burnishing process but this does not make the most of water-gilding, apart from the special effects created by unburnished areas contrasting with burnished highlights described earlier.

Mat gilding is a method usually associated with *oil-gilding*, sometimes called *mordant gilding*. This form of gilding cannot be brought to the bright sheen of water-gilding and the burnisher is not used; nor can it be distressed, although a degree of toning is sometimes applied.

The preparation for oil-gilding is similar to water-gilding but without the same degree of perfection. Quite frequently the first coats of hard gesso are omitted and bole is not always used.

Oil-gilding, unlike water-gilding, requires a non-absorbent surface, so the gesso or bole should be coated with shellac before the oil-size is applied.

The gold-size in this instance is a slow drying oil varnish available in various forms usually designated by the time it takes to dry, which varies from three to forty-eight hours. There is a critical point of tackiness which is most vital in this technique; it is reached sooner, of course, with the fast drying oil sizes, but the time available for laying the leaf is in consequence much shorter – often too much so when a large surface area has to be dealt with. Most gilders work with the forty-eight-hour type which allows preparation of the surface on one day and laying the leaf the next, the requisite tackiness for laying the leaf being maintained for as long as may be required to finish the job.

Acrylic, or polymer, medium is a more recent innovation for oil gilding and has the advantage that the leaf can be laid immediately after the medium is applied. Because it dries so quickly, only small areas at a time are sized and gilded, apart from which the resultant finish appears as good as the more traditional oil-varnish method.

(There is a material now available called acrylic, or polymer, gesso; this, however, is not gesso in the sense discussed in these pages. It may be of interest to artists who work with acrylic colours, but I do not believe it has a place in picture framing, at least where gilding is concerned.)

Transfer gold, called *patent-gold* in the USA, is very much easier to handle than the loose leaf so essential in the technique of water gilding. In oil gilding, transfer gold is well suited for what is sometimes called 'gilding in the wind'. This is the method used for outdoor gilding, for example on the spearheads and escutcheons of the iron railings enclosing the very best banks and institutions. I cannot say that I have seen it used to good effect in fine art picture framing but, for the beginner anxious to pursue his craftsmanship into this most important sphere of picture framing, a very good start might be made using the transfer gold technique described below.

Often it is the gilding that marks the difference between ordinary and fine-art framing, and where a gilt finish is used for framing a painting of importance, anything less than real gold leaf has a singularly inevitable way of debasing the picture.

Many ways of simulating gold leaf have been tried, of which the best and most widely used is the so-called *Dutch metal*, a mixture of brass and bronze powders in leaf form applied in a great variety of ways to most of the commercially available picture-frame mouldings. Although the effect is sometimes remarkably good there is little doubt in my mind that imitation gold is not suitable for framing original paintings of importance and high quality.

As for gold and silver paints, they are quite horrible and can be guaranteed to ruin even the humblest picture or the most amateur painting.

Some tips for the beginner wishing to try the simplest form of transfer gilding are as follows:

Make sure the wood surface of the frame is as smooth as careful sanding can make it.

Use three coats of soft gesso, applying each coat before the last one is quite dry. When the final coat is dry, sand it to a really smooth finish.

Now, instead of using shellac, paint the surface with Venetian red acrylic paint broken down with a little water. When quite dry sand this down to a velvety finish.

Apply a coat of 48-hour oil-size and go home or go to bed!

Lay the leaf as you would apply a transfer, smoothing it into place with the finger tips, and then carefully peel off the tissue. Proceed steadily like this, overlapping the leaves very slightly until the whole surface is laid.

Give the oil-size ample time to 'go off' and then dust off any surplus fragments of leaf with a soft mop brush.

If the moulding has a step, a narrow panel or spoon, or a reeded section, you might try a thin film of oil colour here. Use a colour to suit the picture but deepen it with, say, black if the colour is green, and break down the oil paint with turpentine. Wipe it off again if it does not look good, with a cloth moistened with turpentine, and try again. You may even decide that the residual toning is preferable to the gilded or painted section.

You may well have discovered from this the fascination of gilding, even though it is not to be learnt from a book however lucidly it may be described. If you are interested in mastering the art of gilding, I strongly advise you to attend a course or evening class where you can learn at first hand from expert demonstration.

No alchemist, ancient or modern, has yet succeeded in transmuting base metal (or even plastic) into anything resembling the singular beauty of gold. Yet sadly, gilding is not a flourishing trade or craft and may well be at its lowest ebb for five thousand years. Fortunately, however, there are many people willing to travel far to find a framer able to pursue this ancient and subtle craft.

Examples of water-gilded frames can be seen in the colour illustrations on pages 53 and 64 and on the cover of the book.

8 A miscellany of framing

I have said nothing until now about methods of framing with prefabricated and pre-cut materials specially designed for home assembly and for which no skill (apart from understanding the instructions) is required. It would be pointless to enumerate them all; they are to be found in all art shops in a variety of forms, wood, metal or plastic, and in a range of sizes.

Much ingenuity has gone into the design of these ready-to-assemble framing kits and for those with more enthusiasm than natural dexterity they may well provide the answer to do-it-yourself picture framing.

Most of them follow the current trend of simple angled metal framing using polished aluminium. I doubt whether buying a kit of pre-cut metal framing is any cheaper than having the picture framed in metal professionally, but it would certainly be cheaper than making your own metal frame.

In its simplest form, making a metal frame entails two separate operations: first a simple rebated wooden frame is made and then the four sections of the metal frame are cut and screwed to the outside of the wooden frame so that the mitres are in register without being joined.

The mitres of a metal frame must be cut with a hack-saw instead of a tenon saw and can only be joined together by welding, which requires professional skill and very expensive equipment. Furthermore, without the rebate of the wood moulding there is the problem of securing the glass, picture and backing board into the frame.

There is a metal home-assembly framing kit which overcomes these difficulties to a large extent by the design of the polished aluminium extrusion, which is so shaped that everything is slotted into place and secured by specially fabricated components. Explicit instructions are supplied with these assemblies so I will not discuss them here.

Although metal frames are popular and widely used, I would not advise the amateur to make too serious a foray into this aspect of framing. To achieve a high standard it would be necessary to have access to both welding and high-speed metal polishing equipment, which are definitely only safe in the hands of highly skilled workers. The alternative method of cutting metal angle extrusions and screwing them to a wooden frame, in the hope that the mitred corners will look well without being joined or machine polished, is, I think, over-optimistic except for all but the skilled metal worker.

If you are really keen about metal frames, I would say that a metal-skinned moulding is the best thing to tackle. Although the visible part of the frame is metal, the body of the moulding is of wood so that, insofar as cutting and joining is concerned, it can be treated in exactly the same way as previously described for wood mouldings except that a hack-saw will provide a cleaner mitre than a tenon saw, the teeth of which would soon be blunted by the skin of metal.

Of the numerous forms of 'framing' which dispense with the moulding entirely, the most popular is the method using specially designed spring clips which hold the glass, picture and backing board together in a number of places; from six to ten clips may be used according to the size of the picture. This method may be suitable for displaying a print or drawing of no importance other than its decorative effect and where permanence and conservation are not in question.

The picture, glass and backing board must all be of exactly the same dimension. The glass used for this kind of assembly should have the edges smoothed before use; it is not often realized how dangerously sharp these edges can be. A medium grade whetstone dipped in water is quite effective for rendering the edges of the glass at least less than razor sharp; a few strokes along each of the *eight* edges of the piece of glass will do the trick. Locating indentations are made in the backing board with a bradawl to provide anchorage for the small lugs on the reverse side of the securing clips, and hanging fixtures are fitted to the backing board.

Still on the subject of framing pictures other than fine art, a useful method of permanently laying a picture to a board and providing a protective surface film is with dry-mounting tissue and heat-sealing film.

Dry-mounting tissue is coated on both sides with a resin-based adhesive which is activated by heat at temperatures between 200° and 225° Fahrenheit; the tissue is placed between the picture and the base board which are permanently bonded together when the heat is applied, usually under pressure by means of a special heat-press made for this purpose. Small pictures, such as photographs and the like, can be quite effectively bonded using a domestic electric iron to provide the heat and pressure, but larger items are liable to be spoilt by trapped air bubbles without the even pressure and heat generated by a commercial dry-mounting press, a very heavy and expensive machine designed for professional use. There are lighter models of these machines, but even they are quite expensive for other than professional use and, although excellent for photographic work where large areas are rarely a problem, they are ineffective for picture framing applications. Most professional framers, however, will dry-mount work for a small fee.

Heat-sealing is too tricky for the amateur; the heavy commercial dry-mounting press is essential for this, and much experience is needed to recognize which surfaces can survive the process. Here, the film is coated on one side only with a transparent heat-reactive adhesive which is bonded to the picture surface under heat and pressure. The resultant surface film renders the picture impervious to moisture and dirt and can be claimed to be 'washable'. It need hardly be stressed that nothing but reproduction prints of no intrinsic value should be submitted to this process.

A process known as 'block-mounting' combines both dry-mounting and heat-sealing in one operation. A piece of blockboard or thick wooden panel is cut to the exact size of the print (usually a fairly small reproduction of some popular subject) and the picture is dry-mounted to the blockboard at the same time as its surface is heat-sealed by means of the heat-press.

This procedure might at least provide ideas for the amateur; for example, a picture could be bonded to a wood panel, using any suitable adhesive, and its surface could subsequently be varnished with one of the acrylics specially formulated for paper.

For those who are interested in genuine framing, a word can be said here about old or antique frames. Every week I receive at least one telephone call about restoring and re-gilding old frames and, after many years, I have learned how to avoid the arrival of some huge plaster monstrosity covered in dust and cobwebs, alive with woodworm and literally falling apart. I ask whether pieces have fallen off exposing areas of white. The reply is almost always yes – and I am asked to stick the broken pieces back in place and copy some other missing parts of the 'carving' from the pattern that remains, perhaps touch up the 'gold' a little, and nail up the corners which the central heating has caused to split open. I have to explain the colossal expense of making new plaster moulds, and that, although the frame *is* quite probably over a hundred years old, antiquity, beauty and even profitability are unfortunately not always the same thing; at about this point the enquiry comes easily to its conclusion.

Most of the old frames in general circulation are of plaster composition on a wood base. They were in great vogue during the nineteenth and early twentieth centuries, and to some extent are still admired today. The frame makers of that period could have had little notion of the impermanence of their plaster mouldings, lumps of which are now dropping off at a steadily increasing rate in homes, castles, board-rooms and public places the world over.

I know several artists who collect these frames and soak off the plaster by immersing them in a bath or pond, depending on their urban or rural status, and then spend days, even weeks, sandpapering, painting and wiping, scumbling and goodness knows what else before re-using them to house the work they should have been painting instead of messing about with these horrors! It is true, however, that the wood base of some of these frames can be an interesting shape and of some use.

The only way to remove all the plaster composition (often called 'compo') is by prolonged soaking in cold water and, if the frame is large, the process could conceivably be prejudicial to domestic bliss, since a couple of weeks can be no time at all for really ornate examples. The village or garden pond may indeed be the best answer. When sufficiently soaked, the compo can finally be wiped off and the cleaned wood allowed to dry out.

If, as is usually the case, the corners of the frame have opened up, it will be found impossible to close the gaps because they are never parallel. It is better to use the frame for a smaller painting, taking it apart and 're-shooting' the mitres to the new set of dimensions. As for the finish, I am bound to say that nothing I have seen has ever pleased me other than a real water-gilded surface, which certainly can give new life to some of the nicely shaped mouldings exposed after stripping. Many happy hours are spent by numbers of framers who love to try painted frames, but in my opinion they are rarely successful. If gilding is out of the question, I would suggest the very restrained application of a simple wood stain which can then be waxed – for example, a medium oak stain on the inner and outer sections with a light oak for the panel or spoon section of the moulding.

You may be lucky and come across an old frame with the original ornamentation carved out of the solid wood. Such a frame is a treasure to be lovingly restored and cherished and, if possible, used for a painting appropriate to its style and period. These antique carved frames are rare and valuable and their renovation should only be undertaken by experts.

The rarity of carved frames is indicated by the almost complete absence of discussion on the subject in books such as this one. This is due to the fact that the wonderful craft of picture-frame carving is almost extinct. The few good wood carvers still in existence are quickly gobbled up by the antique furniture trade or are too busy in their own particular field to interest themselves in carving picture frames which few people would recognize or care about. This is not to say that modern hand-carved frames are unobtainable; they can be found, but at enormous expense, and are only for the connoisseur able to afford exactly the right frame for a special and rare work of art.

Round and oval frames are interesting shapes for certain pictures and enjoyed a much greater vogue in the past than they do today, which is perhaps why they impart a somewhat old-fashioned aura to a painting framed in this style nowadays. These frames are beyond the scope of the amateur framer, unless he is a highly skilled woodworker, and are only available in a restricted range of styles and sizes from a few specialized manufacturers using sophisticated machinery. Charming examples of miniature round and oval frames can be found in antique shops; it is not a tragedy if the convex glass is broken or missing, as this type of glass is still produced in the clock and watchmakers industry.

In this final chapter the cleaning and restoration of pictures should be mentioned, if only to point out the hazards of trying your hand at something which requires much training, knowledge and experience. Dreadful things have been done to great works of art throughout the years by even the most highly regarded restorers of their day, and it is indeed foolhardy to link picture-framing with restoration, as is so frequently done, without the necessary trained skills being available.

Nowadays, much more emphasis is placed on conservation than restoration, to the point where restorers prefer the title of conservator or conservationist. Conservation describes what is meant by the care and preservation of works of art, conveying the idea that prevention is better than cure; restoration is the cure or reconditioning process.

To avoid the need for restoration, good and careful framing is the first requisite, using the correct materials as explained earlier. If you have old pictures that are in need of restoration, only expert attention will do. Varnish is the best protection for oil paintings. If they have never been varnished they must be protected with glass, or varnished either by the artist or by someone who understands the correct methods and material for this purpose. Some aspects of cleaning and varnishing are within the scope of the amateur, however, providing he first learns how to recognize the limits of his capabilities. The best answer is to buy a book specializing in this very involved subject.

Much of picture framing, particularly in the amateur do-it-yourself sphere, has little or nothing to do with fine art. Nevertheless, there are many non-professional framers who do handle works of art or material of special personal importance, to whom conservation is immensely important. The professional framer has a serious responsibility for using the materials and methods best suited for the conservation of the work entrusted to him; and the amateur framer too, whether an artist seeking to present his work to its best advantage, or just someone framing a family photograph he hopes will be preserved beyond his own lifetime, has equal reason to care about how the job should be done.

Perhaps you will find, as I have, that within the craft of framing there lies a compelling motive for learning and caring about pictures.

Suppliers

PICTURE FRAME MOULDINGS — Generally available from art shops; there are a large number of suppliers – listed in local directories – many of whom supply direct.

MITRE CUTTERS AND OTHER TOOLS — Several makes and types available – select from a really first-class tool shop.

ADHESIVES
For gluing frames
- UK Evo-stik Resin 'W' from all hardware shops
- US White glue (such as Elmer's or Sobo) or animal hide glue; available in hardware stores.

For bonding fabrics to board
- UK 'Unitak' water-based contact adhesive; from most hardware shops (manufactured by Unibond Ltd, Camberley, Surrey).
- US White glue (such as Elmer's or Sobo) or spray adhesives (manufactured by 3M and Zipatone); available in art supply and hardware stores.

For papers and delicate materials (where conservation is of first importance)
- UK Cellulose Gum 7H4C, made by ICI and obtainable from some hardware and art shops; distributed by Hercules Powder Co. Ltd, 1 Great Cumberland Place, London W1.
- US Rice starch (available from Talas Company, 104 Fifth Avenue, New York, NY 10003).

MOUNTING BOARDS (and gummed gold paper)
- UK Generally available from art shops. The leading manufacturer and supplier is Lawrence & Aitken, Albion Works, Kimberley Road, London NW6 (the only supplier of real conservation board).

MOUNTING BOARDS
(and gummed gold paper)

US Often available through good art supply shops. Conservation or museum mounting board is manufactured by:
Bainbridge & Son, 50 Northfield Avenue, Bldg. 425, Raritan Center, Edison, New Jersey 08817.
Rupaco Paper Corp., 62 Kent Street, Brooklyn, New York 11222.
Process Materials Corp., New Jersey.

Bibliography

Bruce's Son & Company *Victorian Frames, Borders and Trade Cuts.* Dover, New York 1976

Dolloff, Francis W. & Perkinson, Roy L. *How to Care for Works of Art on Paper.* Museum of Fine Art, Boston 1971

Gillon, Edmond V., Jnr. *Decorative Frames & Borders: 396 Examples from the Renaissance to the Present Day.* Dover, London 1973; Peter Smith, Gloucester, Massachusetts 1975

Heydenryk, Henry *Art and History of Frames: An Inquiry into the Enhancement of Paintings.* Kaye & Ward, London 1964; Heinemann, New York 1969

Heydenryk, Henry *Right Frame: A Consideration of the Right and Wrong Methods of Framing Pictures.* Heinemann, London and New York 1969

Keck, Caroline K. *How to Take Care of Your Paintings.* Scribners, New York 1978

Index

Figures in italic refer to illustrations

Acknowledgements

Acknowledgements are due to the following for permission to reproduce the illustrations:
figs 1, 2 and 4, The Trustees, The National Gallery, London; fig. 3, The Courtauld Institute Galleries, London; fig. 5, the Greater London Council as Trustees of The Iveagh Bequest, Kenwood; fig. 6, The Victoria and Albert Museum, London; fig. 8, The Trustees, The Lady Lever Art Gallery, Port Sunlight; fig. 7, The Tate Gallery, London; fig. 31, J. Bensusan-Butt Esq and the New Grafton Gallery, Old Bond Street, London; figs 38, 40, 41, 43 and 45, the artist. The colour illustrations are reproduced by courtesy of A. C. S. Adams Esq, Southampton Row, London (page 53), Browse and Darby Gallery, Cork Street, London and the artist (page 64), and Christopher Clarke Esq (page 57). The cover illustration was taken by Aird Taylor Associates.

I would also like to thank John Bishop for doing most of the drawings; John Ward for the frontispiece; Gallery Photographers Ltd and Connie Kilgore for the photographs in chapters 2–8; and my wife for her help in typing the manuscript.